SEO For 2013

Search Engine Optimization Made Easy

Sean Odom

Christian Habermann

"Less than 5% of all businesses on the Internet use professional SEO services, however of those who use Professional SEO services, they garner 87% of all clicks on the Internet."
--AccuQuality.com's "November 2012 Internet Usage Report"

Learn all the secrets from the pros!

MediaWorks Publishing

SEO for 2013: Search Engine Optimization Made Easy

ISBN-13:9780984860050

ISBN-10: 0984860053

This book is dedicated to:

Sean Odom

All those who spend countless hours in the pursuit of the perfect search engine placement and are willing to share knowledge with their peers. And to those who have helped become who I am today.

Christian Habermann

"My friends and family that have supported me over the years and to all the underdogs out there fighting the good fight. I'd also especially like to thank my mom and dad who have always encouraged me to never stop learning and to simply do what you love."

About the author – Sean Odom

Sean Odom (Sean@SEOForResults.com, in Portland Oregon.) has been in the Information Technology industry for over 25 years and in that time he has written for such publishers as Que, Sybex, Coriolis, Paraglyph Press, and Media Works Publishing.

Sean is well known in the Search Engine Optimization (SEO) industry and has been since 1990 when he first wrote an article entitled, "Optimizing for Searches" in PC Computing Magazine. This started a club which blossomed to over 25,000 members in the late 90's. This club then took on the name "SEO Club" and in 2001 Sean Odom wrote his first book on optimization. Today, many professional publications give Sean Odom credit for starting an entire industry of professionals.

In 2008 his books which he republishes yearly to keep up with SEO advances and changes became a best seller. Today, Sean owns and operates one of the most successful SEO companies. Catering to every size of business he garners results and has contributed to the success of hundred of businesses.

Sean also employs two strategic partners in his business. Michael Monahan and Jason McCormick who in the early 1990's created several search engines and participated in designing the algorithms in use today on many of the major search engines and are themselves successful authors and speakers. Together the three authors work as a team and virtual powerhouse in SEO. Their combined techniques and skills are successfully monitor, detect, and apply search engine algorithm changes to each clients websites to give them their clients great results.

Along with their major accomplishments, Mike and Jason along with other developers have designed an in-house system which allows bots, crawlers, and spiders to scan the Internet on a weekly basis for keyword changes, competition changes, mentions of customers names or domains in social media and blogs, detect optimization and design problems immediately on customer web sites and much more. The system allows every customer to receive a weekly updated report on their SEO standings and compare it to their competition.

About the author – Christian Habermann

Habermann (Christian@AuctusMarketing.com) has been a leader and innovator in the start-up and online marketing world for over 15 years. He started his career in sales working with a successful financial online start up CCBN.com in Boston. He was integral in helping to grow CCBN's Street events product which is used by thousands on Wall Street today. During its heyday, CCBN was one of the largest streamers of audio on the internet due to its webcasting product and was sold to Thomson Financial. He then went to The Yankee Group where he helped lead and grow their enterprise market business in a sales management role. More recently, he has been heavily involved in the startup scene here in Boston which is his true passion along with online brand marketing.

In 2007, he co-founded Consumer United and it recently made the Inc. 500 list and is one of the fastest growing businesses in Boston. Currently, he enjoys running his business, Auctus Marketing, where he thoroughly enjoys helping companies market and grow their businesses online. Christian graduated from St. Lawrence University with honors in History and holds an MBA in marketing from Vanderbilt University. .

Acknowledgements

I need to thank all those who have believed in me over the years and made this book such as success. Even though I have been the bestselling SEO author since 2008 and written over 40 books, it still amazes me to see that there are over 30,000 preordered copies of this book even while I am working on it.

It is truly you the reader that I do this for. I need to thank the entire team that worked together to write, edit, and get this book on the shelves in the limited amount of time we had to do it. My name is on the cover along with Christian Habermann but it took dozens of people, sleepless nights to make our deadlines.

--Sean Odom

TABLE OF CONTENTS

SEO In 2012 Recapped

In 1999, I was president of the Sacramento Cisco Users Group, a group dedicated to getting its member certifications, access to training on routers, switches, and using hardware to give better quality of service(QoS) to web servers and other devices used to access the Internet for large companies.

Nearing the year 2000 we had a almost 1,000 members and we were focused on getting all of our servers and devices compliant for the big Y2K event. If you have been in the computer industry for any length of time I am sure you can remember this. After this we focused on creating web servers and using Cisco devices to make the high traffic websites accessible across multiple servers. This kept the users web experiences fast and friendly but also eliminated a point of failure. If one of the web servers failed another one was there to keep the website up.

Yahoo! Altavista, and AOL were the primary search engines at the time. As members in the group started to learn HTML and creating websites they started to ask what, "How do we do so well with the search engines?"

Early on I had learned about meta tags and putting the words on the page which I wanted to be found for. Really back then it was that simple to optimize your website. The other part was to submit your website to all the search engines one by one by using their submission URL to submit your website over and over until each search engine started indexing your website.

In 2000, I was teaching Cisco and Microsoft certification classes in Plano, Texas the topic turned to the group I represented in Sacramento, what we did and the different topics we addressed. One of the members of the group was Ted Nugent, who at the time was an editor for the then little known PC Computing Magazine. A few weeks after the class was over, I received a call from Ted about wanting me to write an article which explained what needed to be done in HTML to get your website to be found by the search engines.

That article was published in November of 2000 and was titled "Optimizing Your Website For Search Engines", that article was copied, rewritten and posted all over the world. Today most every book and text on Internet history credits me with starting Search Engine Optimization (SEO).

In 2001 I started doing SEO for my clients websites and every year since I have written a book to update those on search engine optimization. Since then I don't think there has ever been a year where there have been more changes to how you need to optimize your website itself, make changes to your pages and update old content on your pages than this past year.

SEO now encompasses not just what is on your pages but what you do off-page (On the Internet) has changed so much as well. This includes social media, link building, and what you need to do to make your website look as though or become an authority in your industry has changed so much as well.

This year it has been a never ending battle and this battle believe it or not is just heating up. Google is both a friend and a foe for businesses using the Internet to market their products or services. To compete, businesses must utilize SEO or die for the most part. Pay-Per-Click (PPC) is just getting more and more expensive and the cost per click is raising faster than the cost of raw materials and eating more and more in to a company's profits.

I have seen so many businesses this past year that relied on PPC instead of SEO take a fall and go out of business. I have also seen businesses who were doing PPC and concentrated money on their SEO have a windfall. You always want to do PPC but concentrate more of your money on SEO. People click on organic results ten times more than PPC. Why do they click on organic results? Because they usually get more relevant information. Anyone can put an ad out in Pay Per Click if they are willing to pay for it. It doesn't even have to be relevant to your search.

Chapter 1 – SEO At A Glance

When people come up to me when I am a speaker at shows or other book signing events, they ask me "What is SEO?". I quickly reply, "No one uses the telephone book anymore, right?" At this point I usually get a nod "yes". Then I continue, "People use Google, Bing or Yahoo! as their telephone book." Then I go on, "If your company's website is not on the first page of Google, Bing, or Yahoo! for a search for your product or service, you are either losing allot of business or your business is going to fail. Search Engine Optimization (SEO) is the exact science to get your website up on page 1 of a search. If your website is on page two or later for the keywords that define your product or service, you are invisible on the Internet."

Almost every company now has a website but less than 5% know of SEO or use Search Engine Optimization (SEO) as part of a marketing plan. This is a big mistake. One of the biggest Internet statistics companies, AccuQuality.com stated in their November 2012 Internet Usage Report that those companies who use professional SEO services garner over 87% of all clicks on the Internet. So if SEO is not part of your marketing plan it should be. Those using PPC a mere 11% of the clicks. Only 2% of the 4 billion business websites out there got traffic from search engines that didn't pay for it with PPC or use SEO.

> **NOTE:** *Statistics from AccuQuality.com report used with signed permission statement.*

To do SEO right you now need to also remember to utilize both Google and Bing's Webmaster Tools as well as Google Analytics. These tools have all changed and been made extremely better with brand new features and changes to the features that already existed as you will learn later in this book.

As I said earlier, the Internet is now the telephone book. So as a business you have to adapt and not only adapt well, but do one better than your competitors so your website URL comes up at the top of the list in any keyword search. No longer can you just pay $2,500 a month for a full page ad in a telephone book to stand out. You have to do the equivalent on the Internet. Your website has to stand out in the center of 4 billion other business websites and outshine all the other competitors in your industry to be successful.

My website looks better than my competition! I'm good, right?

Good SEO does not really care about looks. You want to have a great looking website but you have to incorporate about 150 different coded items that Google and the other search engines look for and the list grows every year. The coding behind the look of your website is actually more important than what your visitors see when it comes to marketing your website to the search engines. That's why some of the ugliest websites make the first page of Google. It really boils down to a task of marketing your website not only to your customers but to the search engines.

Search Engine Algorithms

First off, many do not know what an *algorithm* is and with Google they mistakenly think it is one algorithm when it is actually many with each having a specific task. An algorithm is basically a program that is made to filter data and provide results. I know it may be tough to understand, especially if you have never had any programming knowledge.

Sidebar: How do search engines collect information on websites?

Search engines and Google collect information on every website using little programs called bots, crawlers, or spiders. These little programs have visited virtually every website on the Internet to collect information on everyone of them. These little programs collect keywords, phrases, links, and other coding located on every website. It then stores this information in huge databases used by the search engines. Virtually a copy of every publically available website and picture worldwide can be found on these search engine databases.

To make it easy to understand, imagine that you have a list in an Excel document and it contained 5,000 names and you only wanted to know the names in the list that had the last name of Smith. You could write a small program that found only the name Smith and display those names. That is a basic algorithm. Now Google's algorithms are much more complex and the amount of data it has to filter is almost unimaginable but each algorithm Google runs as a specific task and provides different results.

In 2012, Google used many different algorithms to shake things up. Each algorithm has a specific purpose or filter and each time they run continuously shake things up.

Panda Algorithm

This is a series of algorithms with the specific purpose of filtering based on content or words that are actually seen on the page. It looks for such on-page factors as such as how much content is on a web page, whether the content is duplicated on the same website or on other websites, how often the content is updated, and how much content is on a page.

This is the algorithm that runs and really shakes things up. This has been a very active algorithm in the past two years and we have seen over 20 changes to this algorithm since it was announced.

Penguin Update

This algorithm's primary purpose is to look for over-optimization factors on website pages and other factors such as linking. This algorithm is more of a shakeup algorithm. It runs periodically to shake things up and other algorithms that run later actually reverse most of the effects of this algorithm within two to four weeks.

Penalty Algorithms

These are algorithms that run by Google that penalize websites based on certain criteria. Such as links from porn websites, links from certain identified paid link farms, unnatural link building, negative reviews, negative PR, duplicate content, high bounce rates which can indicate that that visitors are not finding what they were searching for on the website and leave quickly, and many other factors.

Google has many of these and some run just once, some run once a year, and some run about every three months.

Domain Name Match

This is an algorithm we detected in the summer of 2012 and then Google announced the algorithm to scare people from getting or using keyword matching domains. Say you have a roofing company in Miami and people search on Google for "Miami roofing company". To help you in Google's results, you buy the domain name MiamiRoofingCompany.com to help you become relevant for that key term. Google uses this algorithm to make that domain name drop in its results for the keyword.

This is really another algorithm that runs to shake things up. Google wants to be the phone book for the Internet. The problem with this algorithm for Google is that when the algorithm runs, many of the domains that are exact matches are brands and Google has really had to turn this algorithm down.

Manual Intervention

This is something new. It is a process where Google's technical team members can give a manual penalty to a website for just about any reason or take a penalty away. Most are given for bad press or using   paid linking or link farms.

PDF Algorithm

Believe it or not there is an algorithm that gives PDFs with a keyword relevance enough to make it on to the first page.

NOTE: *Each algorithm takes a tremendous amount of processing power and must filter against billions and billions of items in Google's databases. Most only run periodically and some only run a few times a year.*

Algorithm Changes For 2012

At SEO For Results we track algorithm changes using about 180 different websites. We can usually detect and get a determination of what has changed in Google's algorithms with in a very short time. Just so you can get a sense of how often Google changes the different algorithms let's take a look at each months changes.

Panda Update 4.3 - Third Week of December

Just right before the New Year's holidays, Google rolled out another Panda update. They officially called it a "refresh", which they state changed 1.3% of English queries.

Google Knowledge Graph Update - First Week of December

For this Algorithm change Google added Knowledge Graph functionality to non-English queries, Spanish, French, German, Portuguese, Japanese, Russian, and Italian.

Panda Update 4.2 - Third Week Of November

Google confirmed the 22nd Panda update. This came on the heels of a larger, but unnamed update which Google never named on November 19th. Google stated that this effect around .08% of queries.

Panda Update 4.1 - First Week of November

This was Google's 21st Panda attempt to perfect the Panda algorithm change. This officially effected 1.1% of English queries. Several reporting companies are calling this Panda update 2.1 and changing the numbering system.

Page Layout #2 - Second Week of October

Google announced an update to its original page layout algorithm change which occurred in January of 2012. This targeted pages with too many ads "above the fold". If you have too many ads on your page your website page is docked ranking points. Google isn't stupid. They want you to advertise on Google not on your own website or someone else's.

Penguin Update 3.0 - First Week of October

After suggesting the next Penguin update would be a major update, Google actually released a minor Penguin data update which only effected about "0.3% of all queries".

August and September Updates (65 of them)

This was a huge month where we either detected or Google announced more than 65 updates. Google also tested many pages where only 7 organic results displayed instead of the normal 10. There was also Knowledge Graph expansion changes, updates to how "page quality" is calculated, several that changed the way Google local and local results are determined and displayed, a very minor update for Panda the third week of August, and also a penalty for websites accused of digital piracy.

Also Google announced a change in the way it is ranking exact-match domains (EMDs). This led to large-scale devaluation. Google stated this effected about 0.6% of queries. Later we saw a reversal of this effect in Google's results over time.

The last week of September was the Penguin 2.0 and another Panda update which was one of the largest algorithm changes and really shook things up. This officially effected 2.4% of all queries.

June and July Updates (86 of them)

After a slow May, Google made up for it in June and July. Many of the updates effected Panda in updates 3.5, Panda 3.6, Panda 3.7, Panda 3.8, Panda 3.9, ranking fresh content better, a ranking increase for what Google termed "trusted sources",

May 2012 Updates (39 Updates)

In May Google started rolling out "Knowledge Graph". This is a SERP-integrated display providing supplemental objects in the results related to certain people, places, and things. The output in the graphs are officially called "knowledge panels".

This was one of Googles slowest months for updates in quite some time. Also Google released its Penguin Update 1.1, updated link-scheme detection, and an update to TITLE tag requirements. Officially Google admitted to 39 changes this month.

April 2012 Updates (Another 50+)

Google actually published details of 52 different updates in April. This comes after a change that included a mistake in Google's algorithms that target many good websites as being parked domains. This month updates included a new "Penguin" update. This month's updates changes Google's index by over 15%. This is the largest in over a year. The changes to their index targeted improved pagination handling, document ranking, an "Over-optimization penalty", a "Webspam Update" which was somewhat tied to the new Penguin Update, a rewards for good quality websites, and a

Panda 3.5 update. And Google started to send updates on bad links in Webmaster Tools.

March 2012 Updates (50+)

During this month Google made around 50 significant changes to Google's algorithms that ran throughout the month. These changes included a major revision of Panda officially called Panda 3.4, changes to the anchor-text "scoring" method, changes to Navigational Search, several new updates to image search, and changes to how queries for local search are interpreted.

February 2012 Update (35+)

This was a slow month for Google updates when they made only a little over 35 significant changes to their algorithms. Many of the changes related to increasing search speed, image search changes, providing websites with newer content, and but one major and the release of the Panda 3.3 update.

In a release, Google mentioned a new update with the code-name "Venice". This update appeared to make changes to the local search results and how local search was tied to the persons IP address.

January 2012 Updates (40+)

Google Panda 3.2 Update Confirmed (SEL)

During this month we detected around 40 different algorithm changes and Google confirmed in an announcement 30 of them over the month with several receiving codenames. These changes included image search landing-page quality detection, more relevant site-links, changes to rich snippets, "Top Heavy" ad placement, "Megasitelinks", aggressively pushed Google+, Search+ Your World, Panda update 3.2, and search query improvements.

Search Engine Queries

The search query bar is the most familiar part of the search engine. The search query bar is the little box where you type the words related to what you want to find and select a search. In a few moments just like magic, a list of websites shows up on the results screen. Today, the search engines are getting good at giving you the best results possible. It is rare that you will click on an organic link not relevant to your search words or a website that no longer exists. Since the Panda update was released you also won't find many websites without recently updated content.

Now I mentioned organic links in the last paragraph. An organic link is a list of 7 to 10 results on the results page when you type in a search that come up because of the algorithm used by the search engines. Until this year it was standard to see 10 results but Google has been experimenting with pages that have fewer organic results and more paid results.

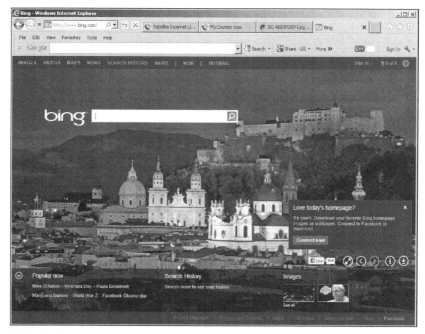

What's interesting is that Bing and Google both know where you are based on your IP Address and other geographical indications.

> **NOTE:** *Google is also getting smarter with personalized results. If you are logged in to Google and you perform the same search multiple times, Google assumes you didn't find the earlier results relevant and gives you a different set of results.*

Now on Google as I am visiting Miami Florida and as I type you can see how Google gives you suggested keywords. This is important later as studies are showing that users chose these suggestions more than 50% of the time as you can see below.

Google

miami computer repair

miami computer repair
miami computer repair **services**
miami computer repair **site**
miami computer repair **genie**

Press Enter to search

You will also notice from the next screenshot that I did not specify any address or whether it was for Miami Florida or the city of Miami in any other state. It only gave me results for computer places in Miami Florida where I happen to be. More important than that, I got computer places just around the hotel I am staying at. It knows this information simply from the IP Address my computer is using to access the Internet. It's absolutely amazing how far search engines have come and how fast their advanced algorithms work.

So now I need to tell you a new term you will see throughout this book with the initials SERP or SERPs. When you type in a string of words to get relevant results and then click search, the collection of pages you see with the results are termed *search engine results pages (SERPs)* in the search engine world. The higher your business or entity is found on search results pages, the more traffic you can expect to generate from searches on those key words.

It has been proven that those in the top 20 get the most clicks, as users typically do not go beyond page 2 of a search. If your website is in the first five results in a search, given that the description you created for your website is enticing to the search, you will get the most clicks for that keyword. Your goal is to get your website at least on page one of the searches. It really is sink or swim. If you are on page one for a search you get all the business in the world. If you are on page two or more you will be virtually invisible. Sales really is a numbers game. If your product or service makes a sale on an average of 1 out of every 10 visitors to your website, the more visits you get the more sales you will make.

Something very interesting has happened with Google this year and the first I heard about this was from AccuQuality.com's Internet Usage Report for 2012 issued in November. This report list major trends and usage behavior and something big caught my eye. Being in the first position of Google for most searches will not land you the most clicks anymore. At first I thought this couldn't be true. The results this year have been astonishing and user behaviors have really changed. Most clicks for almost all keywords on Google based on their research are coming from positions two through six on the first page of SERPs.

There are many reason cited in the report but the most common given by users is Google has done a good job a masking where the PPC results are and the first organic result on Google appears on many video screens as part of the PPC ad group above the page. This is important because many people trust organic results much more than pay-per-click results. About 10 to 1. This means people click on organic results about 90% of the time. Almost anyone can pay money for PPC and many of the PPC ads shown on pages have no relation to their searches as the organic results more often do.

Secondly, many people believe the first website in Google's results are either the most expensive or they are paying Google to be there. This last reason is because the 1st organic result on a SERP is often by itself underneath the PPC but above the Google Products listings or the Local Places results. It creates some confusion.

Chapter 2 – Keywords

Google has said having the keywords in the Keyword Meta tag is no longer a requirement for Google, but they are helpful on other search engines. Google scans the actual relevant content that is on all the pages on your website (with correct linkage that is) and places more weight on the words placed in the <Title> tag and the description. In fact so much weight is now given, you shouldn't place anything other than a single keyword in the Title tag of each page.

> **WARNING:** *We already touched on this a little but for websites that have their relevant content or words mainly in pictures or in Flash the search engine crawlers cannot read this. This is why the most Flashy and spectacular looking websites are on found on page 54 or later in a keyword search.*
>
> *There is now another reason for this. Google has said in the past it is doing better but I certainly haven't seen it. If Google is to rank your website well, you better be compatible with as many browsers and smart phones as possible. The fact is Flash is not compatible with IPods, IPads, IPad Minis, and IPhones so if you have flash on your website...it needs to go.*

Now I said that having the keyword in the Meta tags on Google was not a requirement, but I wouldn't leave them out. If you were looking at this from points prospective, your description, keywords, and other information in your Meta tag all give you more points if they match the content of the actual page of your website. It all adds up to what the search engines see as relevant content and if their algorithms calculate the content as naturally occurring.

Natural occurrence is fairly new to SEO. This is where search engine algorithms look at your website page as well as how often your website is mentioned on the Internet and where. It then compares this statistical information with the search engine algorithm to see if it is natural. We will talk more about this later in the book.

In the next few sections let's take a look at how to choose your keywords. Then let's take a step-by-step look at properly formatting your meta tags to give good information to the search engine spiders and crawlers as well as make the description appealing to a searcher who sees your website in the search results.

The Science Behind Choosing Keywords

Keywords are one of the most important elements of your website. In fact before you start optimizing your website you need to choose the keywords. Now, the keywords you choose today maybe completely different than the keywords you optimize for a year from now. That is if you are doing proper SEO and tracking your results.

That last sentence might have really got people scratching their heads so I better explain. Google is getting really good at getting people to use Adwords. Part of their overall strategy to get people to do this is to change the way people search. How you ask? Well over 60% of those searching Google get keyword suggestions when they perform a search. This means when the person starts to type their search in Google's search bar they get suggested keywords as they type. They then can just select one of the keywords instead of continuing to type their search phrase.

So if today you decide that you want to redesign your kitchen and you go to Google looking for a kitchen design company you might start by typing "kitchen" and you may get some keyword suggestions. The suggestion today might be "Kitchen Remodel". The suggestion six months from now might be "Kitchen Renovation" or "Kitchen Remodeler". It changes up the pages you should optimizing for at the current time.

My recommendation to my clients is to add a new optimized page for the new keyword in case Google ever goes back and not modify the currently ranking page with the old keyword. Which most likely Google will eventually go back to the previous suggested keywords. You are however starting to get the reasoning behind me stating that the keywords you focus on today may be different or added to later on.

When choosing the best keywords to focus on for your website there is a simple rule. Good research gets you good results.

You can start off with the basics of searching for keywords and use the Google Adwords Keyword Tool which is free for all to use. But this is Google's suggestions and not necessarily what people will search for all the time.

> *TIP:* *There are other third party tools you can use to determine the best keywords. You can use services such WebsiteSubmitter.org, SubmissionComplete.com, or SEOAudits.com.*

Google has this tool not just for suggestions, but the more people they have vying for the same keywords, the higher the going rate per click for each of those keywords is going to be. Adwords click price is ruled by bidding on the keywords and the people willing to pay the most amount of money usually end up on top. There are some variations to that rule such as ad quality but for the most part, the person willing to pay the most per click ends up on top.

You can get to the Google Keywords tool from two URLs. They are:

https://adwords.google.com/o/KeywordTool

http://www.googlekeywordstool.com

By entering a search phrase in Google Adwords Keyword Tool you can see what sort of competition you are up against. You can see from the screenshot below you can also have it look at your website and give you some keyword suggestions. I have used this before and very rarely does it give me the relevant keywords unless the website has already been optimized for the keywords.

Notice that I have chosen to look for the keyword kitchen renovation. I happen to have allot of experience in the kitchen and bath industry over the years.

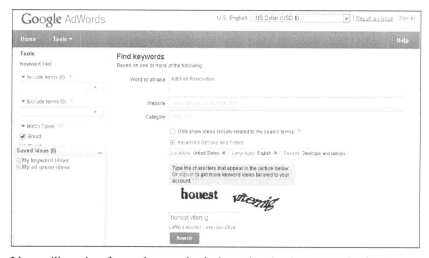

You will notice from the results below that it gives you the basic keywords that people search for. The Competition Level indicates how hard it is not only to rank for that keyword but also is a good indicator of how much competition there is. The higher the Competition Level indicator is, the more your likely to pay for Pay-Per-Click for that term to get on page one and the more you're going to have to do in SEO terms to get ranked on the first page for that keyword term.

Every business owner who has a website wants to rank highly for the keywords with high competition. If your new to SEO and your just trying to do SEO or trying to rank a new website, you're going to be sorely disappointed that you won't rank well or be seen for a while. I recommend if you are new to SEO or you have a new website that you try and find combinations of keywords that return pages with "POOR" competition scores. If you can write and optimize a page of content using one or more "POOR" keywords you should be able to rank highly in searches and get at least some visits and traffic to your website quickly. That is provided that you follow the basics of search engine optimization.

Keyword	Competition		Global Monthly Searches ?	Local Monthly Searches ?
☐ kitchen renovation ▾	High		110,000	60,500

☐ ✓ Save all	**Keyword ideas (100)**		1 - 50 of 100 ▾	‹ ›

	Keyword	Competition	Global Monthly Searches ?	Local Monthly Searches ?
☐	kitchen renovation ideas ▾	High	6,600	2,400
☐	kitchen renovations ▾	High	110,000	74,000
☐	kitchen renovation cost ▾	High	8,100	4,400
☐	cost of kitchen renovation ▾	High	8,100	4,400
☐	small kitchen renovations ▾	High	1,900	1,000
☐	kitchen renovations ideas ▾	High	5,400	1,600
☐	small kitchen renovation ▾	High	2,400	1,300
☐	kitchen renovation costs ▾	High	5,400	3,600
☐	kitchen renovation budget ▾	High	1,300	590
☐	kitchen renovation photos ▾	High	1,000	480
☐	cheap kitchen renovation ▾	High	1,000	390
☐	kitchen renovation tips ▾	High	590	260
☐	kitchen renovation pictures ▾	High	1,000	480
☐	kitchen design ▾	High	1,000,000	368,000
☐	kitchen remodel ▾	High	201,000	201,000

TIP: *There are two subscription based keyword suggestion tools you can use for keyword results if you want to pay money for them that I recommend. They are the keyword tools from RavenTools.com and SEOMOZ.com. They won't do the work for you. Just give you a second or third list of keywords Google might not give you.*

The keywords in the results that Google gives you are the keywords that Google considers related to the term you searched for. Many times it will not cover all the bases and give you all the keywords you should be focused on. The next step is to brainstorm new keyword ideas based on whatever the topic is that your website focuses on. It can be model numbers, part numbers, product descriptions, etc. Keyword terms can also come from you sitting in the driver's seat and thinking, if you were the person searching for what you have to offer, what would you search for?

Ignore the results Google tries to give you and think for yourself. You can also look at your competitions website or use KeywordSpy.com to see what your competition optimizes their website for. These are all great ways to find some of the less competitive keywords to focus on.

Now that we have learned how to search and get the suggested keywords we probably have a list a mile long. You haven't learned this yet but every keyword you choose has to have its own page, written text focusing on the keyword, get links built for the page, and social media targeting it. So you are going to want to narrow this list down to a smaller list which we call our trophy keywords

We already know the possible keywords, the number of local and global searches, and an estimate of how much competition there are for those keywords. So where do we go from here?

I spend countless hours finding and applying the right keywords for my customers and finding the most effective keywords is a science and sometimes it's an experimental process. If you have a newer website it's pretty easy, take the "POOR" rated keywords, find the ones that are most relevant to what you sell or do and focus on the most searched for first.

If you have a website that is already ranked or you are over 6 months in to your SEO campaign you have to look at the keyword list from Google that you got from the last few pages differently. You have to weigh heavily searched on keywords against the amount of competition the keyword has. If you have a high Google ranking for your website or webpage you can compete against whoever you want for the keywords that have a much higher competition score.

If I went right out for the search term "Kitchen Renovation" as shown in previous screenshot, there are 8000 sites ranked higher than a brand new website which has a Google ranking of "0". It's pretty hard to get on to page 1 for that. However, if your website or website page has a ranking of "3" or more your competition narrows to about 200 websites. If only about 5% use any professional SEO or keep up with the latest SEO techniques you are looking at only about 10 competitors. Your now seeing how ranking and optimization play a role with search engines.

If your website or website pages already has a Google Ranking of "2" or more then you can start focusing on "MEDIUM" or "HIGH" competition keywords. If this is the case you can use this formula: Choose only the keywords that have the most amount of searches to optimize first and work your way down to lower searched keywords until you have either exhausted your ability to create new keyword pages or you are getting too many to do links and social media for.

If you have a newer website or are just starting SEO stick to the simple rule of choosing keywords with the highest amount of searches and the lowest amount of competition. You kind of have to meet in the middle of competition score versus searches.

Long Tail Keywords

Long tail keywords are keyword phrases that have at least two, and some times as many as five descriptive words in the phrase. Just like normal keywords, long tail keywords are used to define what is on the web page and what the searcher wants to more specifically find. Long tail keywords are more specific, and tend draw less traffic for the website, but tend to draw more quality traffic. Visitors to your website use long tail keywords to narrow down what they are searching for. When a potential visitor is looking to remodel their kitchen in Baltimore, if they just searched for "Kitchen Remodel" they might get results from all over the country and not local. A user might create a more refined long tail keyword search such as "Baltimore Kitchen Remodeling Company" to get more specific results. You have to take that in to account and optimize for that keyword combination as well.

To know what long tail keywords to focus on, research is basically the only way to know what keywords will work or not. A small investment of time and effort will pay off in the end. Longer tail keywords always have a much lower competition score and if your website focuses on a local geographical area you need to always include the city and keyword and vice versa for the keywords you focus on.

Now that we have an understanding of the keywords we are going to use, the first step is to create a page for each keyword and setup the Meta Tags and the Title for each one of those pages you are optimizing.

Creating The Meta Data For Each Page

We already learned earlier in the chapter that that our Meta tagging starts with determining our keywords. I am going to create an imaginary company focusing on the kitchen renovation since I have already been using that throughout the whole chapter.

Let's call our imaginary business called Kitchen Remodeling Experts and say it is in Baltimore, Maryland. We need a domain name so we will say our domain is KitchenRemodelingExperts.com which will probably be available until the first kitchen and bath company owner reads this book. It's a premium domain and I am surprised it is available still.

I also did a Google search to make sure it wasn't really a business to. So if it becomes one after this book and they trademark it, well guess what, you can't sue me for using it as I had the first use of the name. I say that because in my last two books I created an imaginary company and someone took the name, started a company, used the domain, and is using the exact Meta tagging I created for the books. So I guess for this one it will be first come, first serve again.

So my imaginary company needs some keywords. So based on my analysis the most sought after and highly competitive keywords are:

- Baltimore Kitchen Renovation
- Baltimore Kitchen Remodeler
- Baltimore Kitchen Remodeling
- Baltimore Kitchen Ideas
- Baltimore New Kitchen

I actually came up with about 50 more keywords but these are the most basic. Also if this were a real company I would also use all the keywords with Washington DC and DC as along with the city of Baltimore as it is so close.

So let us take a look at what I came up with for the title and Meta tagging for this website. After I show you the Meta Tag I will break each line down so you know how to choose each lines specific text.

```
<HEAD>
<Title>Baltimore Kitchen Remodeling</Title>
```

```
<Meta http-equiv="Content-type" content="text/html; charset=ISO-
8859-1">
<Meta name="keywords" content="baltimore kitchen remodeling">
<Meta name="description" content="We are the best Baltimore
kitchen remodeling company. Call us today or you may pay too
much!">
<Meta name="googlebot" content="index, follow" />
<META http-equiv="Content-Language" CONTENT="EN-US">
<Meta name="robots" content=" index, follow ">
<Meta name="Revist-After" content="7 days">
<Meta name="city" content="Baltimore">
<Meta name="country" content="United States (USA)">
<Meta name="state" content="MD">
<Meta name="zip code" content="21201">
<Meta name="subject" content="Baltimore Kitchen Remodeling">
<Meta name="author" content="Kitchen Remodeling Experts">
<Meta name="copyright" content="Kitchen Remodeling Experts">
</HEAD>

<Body>
(This is where the visible portion of your website is configured.)
</Body>
```

Take a look at each one of these in the next sections.

Configuring the Keyword Meta Tag

The order that you place META data on the page is actually unimportant and to help this make sense to you I am changing the order I explain it a little bit. First off, there is a misconception. I am going to tell you keywords are IMPORTANT. You shouldn't even think about the Title tag or the Description tag until you have decided on the keyword the page is going to focus on.

You already learned the science behind carefully choosing your keywords. So once you know the keyword you are assigning to the page, the tag is configured like this:

```
<Meta name="keywords" content="baltimore kitchen
remodeling">
```

I made keywords bold for this example but the keyword is not bolded in the configuration. You might notice something else. All the keywords are in lower case. Why? Well Google doesn't care, but we need to think about all the search engines. Some search engines are case sensitive and most people don't capitalize their word searches. They just type in their keywords to search.

Configuring the Meta Title Tag

The *Title Tag* is used to define the title of a web page, with the Title tag placed between the <head> and </head> tags in the html of the page. Search engines will recognize the Title tag as the title of the page. Each page should have its own distinct Title tag.

It is recommended that you keep your Title Tag short, with no more than 70 characters. Don't use irrelevant words (meaning words that are not found on the page) in your Title will dilute the impact on your targeted keywords.

This is where Google typically learns the keyword it is looking for on the page. Google does not use the keywords tag for this like other search engines it uses the TITLE tag. There should never be anything in this tag other than the keyword for the page.

<Title> **Baltimore Kitchen Remodeling**</Title>

Configuring the Description Tag

The maximum length of a displayed description varies between search engine. In creating the description, try to place your most important keywords early in your Description tag, in case the search engine truncates the results. Your wording should always include a hint at a call to action such as "Call us first" or "Save money with us! Come in today."

Keep your Description between 50 and 149 characters, including spaces, whenever possible. Google will display 154 characters, but other search engines display less. Longer descriptions are of little value, as most search engines place little to no importance on this tag.

Configuring the GoogleBot and the Robot Tags

Here is the Meta Robots tag that we discussed a few sections back in a sidebar. You might notice another tag though. Google really likes it when you put its own Meta tag in your website and tell them what to do. That tag is called "googlebot" and the instructions are similar to the Robots tag as shown:

index: This allows the GoogleBot to index that page.

noindex: This tells the GoogleBot not to index the page.

follow: This allows the GoogleBot to follow the links from the landing page and other pages it finds and index them.

nofollow: This instructs the spider not to follow links from that page for indexing.

Noodp: Prevents the search from using the page's description.

The tags are easy and should be in any website you have. Also, you never know what users or links Googlebot or other creepy crawlers arrive from and so these should be in the Meta tags of every page in your website.

<Meta name="googlebot" content="**index, follow**" />
<Meta name="robots" content=" **index, follow** ">

Language Identifier

<META http-equiv="Content-Language" CONTENT="**EN-US**">

The Language META tag declares to the search engines the natural language of the document being indexed. Search engines which index websites based on language often read this tag to determine which language(s) is supported. This tag is particularly useful for non-English and multiple language websites. It also helps Google to determine which or how many of its different county search engines it should list the website page.

The different choices for this tag are:

BG (Bulgarian)
CS (Czech)
DA (Danish)
DE (German)
EL (Greek)
EN (English)
EN-GB (English-Great Britain)
EN-US (English-United States)
ES (Spanish)
ES-ES (Spanish-Spain)
FI (Finnish)
HR (Croatian)
IT (Italian)
FR (French)
FR-CA (French-Quebec)
FR-FR (French-France)
IT (Italian)

JA (Japanese)
KO (Korean)
NL (Dutch)
NO (Norwegian)
PL (Polish)
PT (Portuguese)
RU (Russian)
SV (Swedish)
ZH (Chinese)

Configuring the Meta Revisit Tag

Google and other major search engines typically visit your site once per month on average. But let's say your website's content changes more frequently such as a news website? How do you tell the search engines spiders, bots and crawlers to visit more frequently? The "Revisit-After" Meta tag is used just for this purpose.

<Meta name="Revist-After" content="**7 days**">

Configuring the Meta Location Tags

These tags are really important to search engines to help identify the local geographical locations. In the example below, we add the city, country, state, and zip code, just as if you were mailing yourself a letter as shown below:

<Meta name="city" content="**Baltimore**">
<Meta name="country" content="**United States (USA)**">
<Meta name="state" content="**MD**">
<Meta name="zip code" content="**21201**">

Configuring the Meta Subject Tag

This tag arguably has very little influence with the major search engines but it does have some with smaller ones. I typically place the first long tail keywords in my Meta Keywords tag here which should be the most important subject of our website as shown below.

<Meta name="subject" content="**Baltimore Kitchen Remodeling**">

Configuring the Author and Copyright Meta Tags

These two tags do very little to enhance your search engine rankings and have more to do with identifying who owns all the hard work you put in to your website. I see parts of my books in other books and on the Internet all the time. Most have the common sense to give me credit, but when they don't, I get upset. I spent blood, sweat, and tears to get this done. Not to mention the time I didn't get to spend with my family because I was writing and doing other things.

The "author" tag is the person or company name that created the content in the website. The "copyright" tag identifies who owns the copyright. I will remind all the readers that Kitchen Remodeling Experts is entirely bogus and at the time of this writing and they didn't really exist.

So your meta tag when you get done should look like this!

<Meta http-equiv="Content-type" content="text/html; charset=ISO-8859-1">
<Meta name="keywords" content="**baltimore kitchen remodeling**">
<Meta name="description" content="**We are the best Baltimore kitchen remodeling company. Call us today or you may pay too much!**">
<Meta name="googlebot" content="**index, follow**" />
<META http-equiv="Content-Language" CONTENT="**EN-US**">
<Meta name="robots" content=" **index, follow** ">
<Meta name="Revist-After" content="**7 days**">
<Meta name="city" content="**Baltimore**">
<Meta name="country" content="**United States (USA)**">
<Meta name="state" content="**MD**">
<Meta name="zip code" content="**21201**">
<Meta name="subject" content="**Baltimore Kitchen Remodeling**">
<Meta name="author" content="**Kitchen Remodeling Experts**">
<Meta name="copyright" content="**Kitchen Remodeling Experts**">
</HEAD>

Wordpress META Data

Google loves Wordpress more than any other platform. It optimizes easier, indexes faster and for the most part is easier to rank than any other platform. So how do you enter all the Meta info? I recommend ALL IN ONE SEO plug-in for the meta tagging.

You can put in the TITLE, Keywords and the Description Meta Tags at the bottom of each page when you create them in WordPress. Google requires less of WordPress and that is all the information you need in your tagging.

Choosing Quality Keywords

Targeting your trophy keywords is absolutely important!

It's complicated I know. As I said earlier, keywords in Meta tags are no longer a requirement. When I say it is not a requirement, I see companies with a ranking of one or two on Google all the time that do not have a single Meta tag, nor a list of keywords and no description either.

Their domains longevity, linkage, and relevant content sped them along in the process to get ranked. But it won't get them much farther in the ranking process. Each stepping stone that you make on the list gets you a little higher in the ranking process.

I always like to explain it to customers that each item you do equals a point value to the major search engines.

- Have a website that has been online for a long period (Years), add points.
- Have your website registration paid so it expires in 5 years or more, add points.
- Create your website in WordPress get points. (Google seems to love WordPress more than any other web development platform.)
- Have it expire in less than a year, subtract points.
- Have Meta Tags, add points.
- Have relevant content, add points, have quality and relevant links, add points.
- Have an SEO company that is a Search Engine Ambassador, add points.
- Have a good hosting speed add points. (You can check at **http://pagespeed.googlelabs.com**. A passing score is 70 or more.)
- Have a homepage that has is smaller than 180KB get points.

40

- Have news articles published about your website on websites that are determined by Google to be "Official News Sites" such as LocalNewsDay.com, DailyTrib.com, ChicagolandNewspaper.com, FoxNews.com, etc., add a lot of points.
- Have links from .gov and .edu sites, add points.
- Have a good website quality score, add points. (You can check this by employing **SEOAudits.com** or **AccuQuality.com**.)
- Do well on all 130+ factors I outline here in this book, get higher rankings!

The higher the point values, the higher the rankings can become. The more points needed is based on a number of factor, including the industry you're in, the competition you have, competing companies with SEO vying for the top spots, local or national campaigns, traffic to your website, two way links, and much more, but obviously not based on your keywords alone. In fact, it barely has an impact on rankings.

Chapter 3 - What do I need to do first for SEO?

You have a website that is live on the Internet, you have the Meta Tags on like we talked about in the last chapter, you have the keywords chosen and pages dedicated to each keyword. But no one is coming. What needs to be done first? Well you need to tell the world. But you cannot just jump in to building links and doing social media. This all helps and might drive a little traffic but not the numbers you want. You first have to tell the biggest search engine, Google about your website.

After you tell Google, you need to tell the smaller search engines about it, get listed in directories, make sure your mechanics are good, and if you have a brick and mortar location you want to make sure you show up on all the GPS's.

This is allot to cover and I am going to give you some SEO company secrets and shortcuts to help you out. And believe it or not this is all very inexpensive to do. In fact I will include a step later where you go to http://www.SubmissionComplete.com and submit your web site to the 200+ little search engines and another 500 or so directories for about $35.00. This will save you about 100 hours of your precious time, if not more trying to get listed on all the search engines. It is kind of a little secret good SEO's use.

First off, you will want to go to Google and create a Google account for Google Webmasters.

Adding Your Website to Google Webmaster Tools

Google Webmaster Tools is the primary way that Google communicates with webmasters. It provides great traffic data and insight about your site, helps you to identify issues with your site and even lets you know if your site has been infected with malware. Simply start by going to

www.google.com/webmasters/tools/

To start using Google's Webmaster Tools you have to verify that you are an authorized representative of your site. This is done through a process of verification.

How to Add and Verify A Site:

1. Sign into Google Webmaster Tools with your Google Account.

2. Click the **Add a site** button, and type the URL of the site you want to add. Make sure you type the entire URL, such as **http://www.example.com/**

3. Click **Continue**. The **Site verification** page opens.

4. (Optional) In the **Name** box, type a name for your site (for example, **My Blog**).

5. Select the verification method you want, and follow the instructions.

Verification Process

There are four methods of verification and there's no real preference as to which method you use. Here are the four ways:

- **The HTML file upload.** Google provides you with a blank, specially named file that you just have to drop in the root directory of your site. After you do this, just click on the verify button and you will have access to your Google Webmaster Tool data for this site.

- **Adding a HTML tag.** Clicking on this option will provide you with a Meta tag that you can insert into the head of your home page. Once it's there click on the verify button to view your Google Webmaster Tool data.

- **The Google Analytics option**. If the Google account you're using for Google Webmaster Tools is the same account as your Google Analytics and you're using the asynchronous tracking code (with the code being in the head of your home page), then you can verify the site this way.

- **The DNS Method.** Select your Domain Name provider from the drop down list and Google will give you a step by step guide for verification along with a unique security token for you to use.

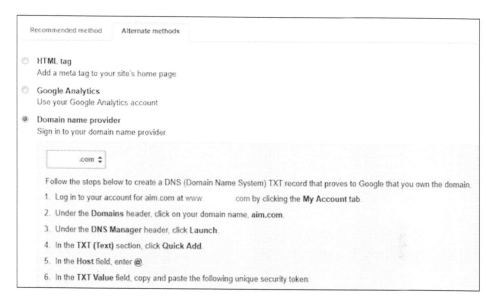

When you login to Google webmaster tools you will get a screen which lists all the domains you have associated with your account.

If you see a red exclamation mark next to a domain, it indicates that there is a problem with the website and you need to look at the message to see what issue Google has found.

Google Webmaster Tools Dashboard

Once you have completed the verification process, you can log in and start to examine the data for your site. If you have just one domain, the Dashboard is the first screen you will be taken to. This gives you a quick view into some of the more pertinent information for your site, along with any new messages you may have from Google.

45

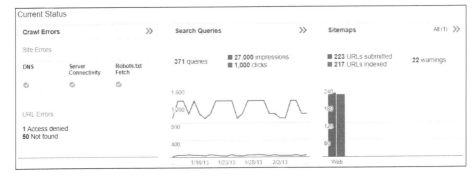

Here is where you receive messages about your site from Google. There may be messages that inform you that your site has pages infected with malware/spam, or just an informational message that your WordPress installation really needs to be updated. Please note, you can also have your messages forwarded to any email address associated with your Google account.

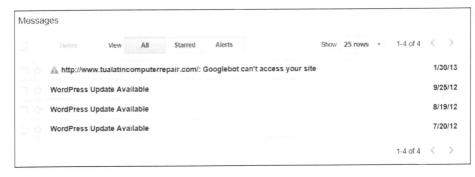

Configuring Webmaster Tool Settings

Here you can tell Google some basic things about your site. For example, you can inform Google of the geographic location your site is targeting, your preferred domain (eg. www.yoursite.com or yoursite.com), and even the crawl rate. Please note the preferred domain option just informs Google whether you want the site to show up in the search results with the www. or without the www. Most sites will redirect from one to the other. The crawl rate option allows you to slow down the rate of Google's spider. If your server is slowed down due to Google's spider, then this may be a wise option, otherwise it's best to keep it as is.

Settings

Geographic target

☐ Target users in: United States ▾

Preferred domain

◉ Don't set a preferred domain
○ Display URLs as **www.computerservicesportland.com**
○ Display URLs as **computerservicesportland.com**

Crawl rate

◉ Let Google optimize for my site **(recommended)**
○ Limit Google's maximum crawl rate

Sitelinks

If your site is an authority on a particular subject which is determined by Google, then Google will display links below your site in the search results.

Breaking News and Opinion on The **Huffington Post**
www.huffingtonpost.com/ +1
Offers syndicated columnists, blogs and news stories with moderated comments.

Entertainment
Get breaking news from the entertainment industry to learn ...

Crime
Get the latest on crime and justice. Follow missing person cases ...

Politics
Follow American politics, keep up with the hottest political debates ...

The Blog
Why is it that we believe we can feed our bodies industrial ...

Weird News
Whether it's weird, funny or bizarre we've got news stories on dumb ...

Style
... fashion industry with news on the latest fashions and celebrity ...

These links point to what Google deems to be the most important links on your site's page. Sometimes Google will show a link that you don't particularly want to be displayed in the search results, and this is where you can demote that link so that it won't appear. Simply enter the URL of the page with the sitelinks (not always just the homepage), and then type in the URL of the sitelink that you want to be removed.

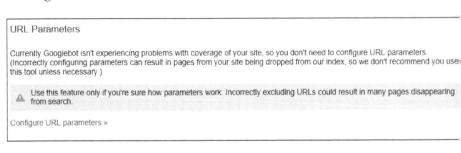

Please note, a demoted link may reappear in your search results after 90 days, so be sure to check this section.

Setting URL Parameters

This feature allows you to specify URL query string parameters that shouldn't be considered when examining URLs on the site to determine unique URLs. For example, if you had a tracking parameter that you use for a particular campaign, then the page is obviously the exact same page as when it's reached without the tracking parameter. Entering the tracking parameter in here tells Google that they should ignore the tracking parameter when looking at the URL.

URL Parameters

Currently Googlebot isn't experiencing problems with coverage of your site, so you don't need to configure URL parameters. (Incorrectly configuring parameters can result in pages from your site being dropped from our index, so we don't recommend you use this tool unless necessary.)

⚠ Use this feature only if you're sure how parameters work. Incorrectly excluding URLs could result in many pages disappearing from search.

Configure URL parameters »

Change of Address

If you change your entire site to a new domain, then this is where you let Google know. Once you've set up your new site, 301'd the content from your old site to your new, added and verified your new site on Google Webmaster Tools, then you inform Google of the move here. Basically, this helps Google's index be updated a little quicker.

Change of Address

Tell Google when you move your site to a new domain. Guidelines for moving your site.

First:

1. Set up your content on your new domain.
2. Redirect content from your old site using 301 redirects.
3. Add and verify your new site to Webmaster Tools.

Tell us the URL of your new domain

www.friscolocalnews.com has moved to: Select a verified site... ⬍   Submit

Creating Users

This is where you can view and control all authorized users on your account. For example, a new user can be added here and you can set their level of authorization. Owners have permission to access every item on the site. Users with "Full" permission can do everything except add users, link a Google Analytics account and inform Google of a change of address. Users with "Restricted" permission have the same restrictions as those with "Full" permission plus the following: they only have viewing capabilities on configuration data, cannot submit sitemaps or request URL removals, cannot submit URLs, cannot submit reconsideration requests, and only have the capability to view crawl errors and malware notifications.

Associates

This section allows you to associate different Google accounts with your GWT account, so that they can be designated as officially connected to the account/site. This is available for sites that are in the YouTube Partners Program and the Chrome Web Store. To associate an account simply click on the "Add a New User" red button, enter the email address that's associated with the YouTube or Chrome Web Store account you're associating, click the appropriate checkbox and hit the add button.

Crawl Errors

Here's where you find out about the errors that Google has detected when crawling your site. This is an invaluable tool as it can absolutely help you identify a variety of issues on your site, from server errors to missing pages, and more. This tool shows you the number of errors, lists the pages and even shows a graph of your error count over time so you can easily see whether it's been a gradual change or a more sudden occurrence. This is a good tool to keep tabs on frequently so that you catch these errors as they crop up.

View messages for http://beautifulkitchensblog.com/ »

↩   Delete

⚠ **http://beautifulkitchensblog.com/: Googlebot can't access your site**

Over the last 24 hours, Googlebot encountered 1 errors while attempting to access your robots.txt. To ensure that we didn't crawl any pages listed in that file, we postponed our crawl. Your site's overall robots.txt error rate is 100.0%.

You can see more details about these errors in Webmaster Tools.

Crawl Stats

This section simply provides you with an idea of how fast the crawlers are able to read your pages. Please note that spikes are to be expected here, but if you see a sustained drop in pages crawled, or a sustained spike in time spent downloading a page, or in the size of a page, then this tells you that you should take a look at what's changed recently on your site.

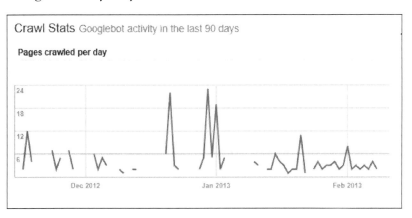

Crawl Stats Googlebot activity in the last 90 days

Pages crawled per day

Blocked URLs

This is where you can test out your current robots.txt on any pages on your site to verify whether they can be crawled or not. You also have the ability to test out modifications to your robots.txt to see whether they will work as you anticipate against various pages on your site.

robots.txt file	Blocked URLs ⊘
http://www.tualatincomputerrepair.com/robots.txt	0

robots.txt analysis

Value
Line 5: Sitemap: http://www.tualatincomputerrepair.com/sitemap.xml.gz

http://www.tualatincomputerrepair.com/robots.txt content - edit to test changes

```
User-agent: *
Disallow: /wp-admin/
Disallow: /wp-includes/

Sitemap: http://www.tualatincomputerrepair.com/sitemap.xml.gz
```

Fetch as Google

This function allows you to view your pages as Google sees them. This tool is designed to help webmasters troubleshoot potential issues with the crawling of their site. It will return the HTTP response, the date and time, and the HTML code, including the first 100kb of visible text on the page. This is a great way of verifying that the Google crawler sees the page as you expect it. If the page looks how you expect it to, then you can submit it to the index. You are allowed 500 fetch submissions per week, and 10 linked page submissions per week.

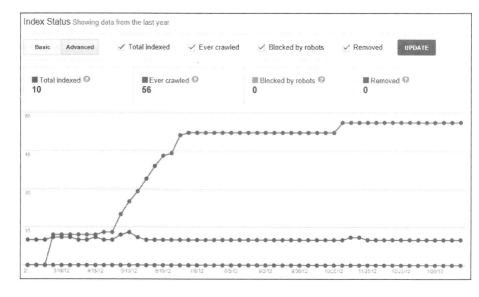

Fetch as Google

Fetches remaining:
499

URL and linked pages
submissions remaining:
10

http://www.tualatincomputerrepair.com/　　　　　　　　　　　Web ⌄　[FETCH]

Leave URL blank to fetch the homepage. Requests may take a few minutes to process.

Show　25 rows　⌄

URL	Googlebot type	Fetch Status	
http://www.tualatincomputerrepair.com/	Web	⊙ Success	Submit to index

Index Status

The Index Status page provides stats about how many of your URLs Google was able to crawl and/or index. A steady increase in the number of crawled and indexed pages indicates that Google can regularly access your content, and that your site is being indexed. If you see a sudden drop in the number of indexed pages, it may mean that your server is down or overloaded, or that Google is having trouble accessing your content. This is definitely an area that you will want to consistently monitor.

Malware

If Google has detected any malware/spam on your site then it will be displayed here. Please note that you will also be notified of this in your messages. If you see a page listed here then you will want to get it fixed as soon as possible and click on the "Request a Review" button that will be displayed here.

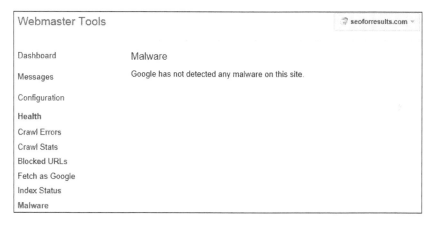

Traffic Search Queries

This page gives information about Google Web Search queries that have returned pages from your site. In addition, you can also see information about the pages on your site that were seen most often in search results (top pages). Hence, you can get an overview of the top keywords that returned a page from your site in the search results. Note the data shown here is collected in a slightly different way from your analytics platform, so don't expect the number to exactly tally. What this does is give you an idea of the top traffic driving keywords for your site, the number of impressions and clicks, and therefore the click through rate (CTR), and the average position that your page was ranking for that particular query.

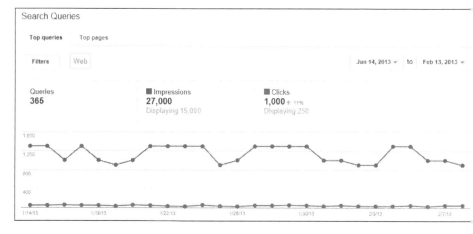

You can also view the same data by page rather than by keyword. This shows you the top traffic generating pages on your site, and perhaps help you identify those that you should concentrate on optimizing, as a high traffic generator in 11th position would be a much higher traffic generator in 8th.

Links to Your Site

This section displays the domains that link to your site the most and your most linked to content. Please note that you can also attain this data if you went to Google.com and performed a search for "Link: yoursite.com", but this section will display more so it is very informative.

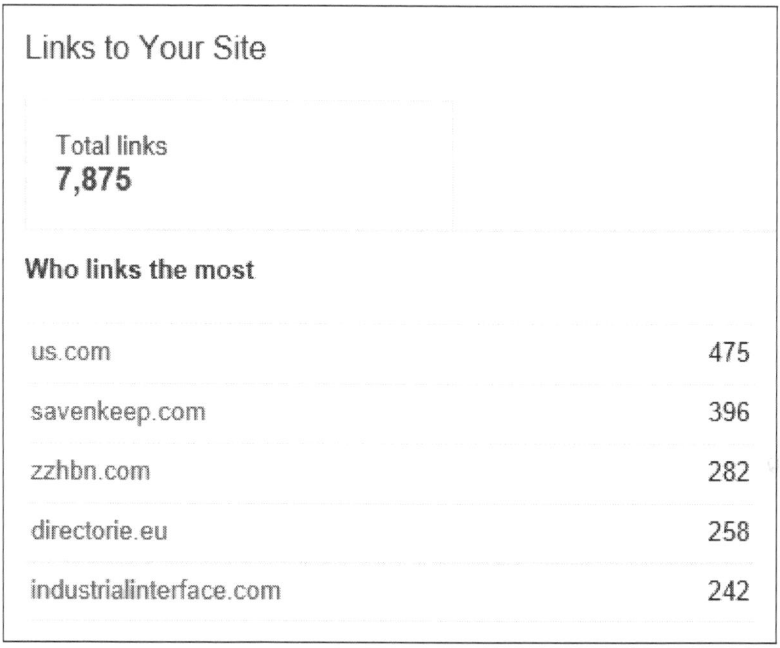

Links to Your Site

Total links
7,875

Who links the most

us.com	475
savenkeep.com	396
zzhbn.com	282
directorie.eu	258
industrialinterface.com	242

Internal Links

The Internal Links page lists a sample of pages from your site that have incoming links from other internal pages. The number of internal links pointing to a page is a signal to search engines about the relative importance of that page. This serves as an indicator of your authority on a subject as well as provides you with a glimpse of a page that Google deems as important.

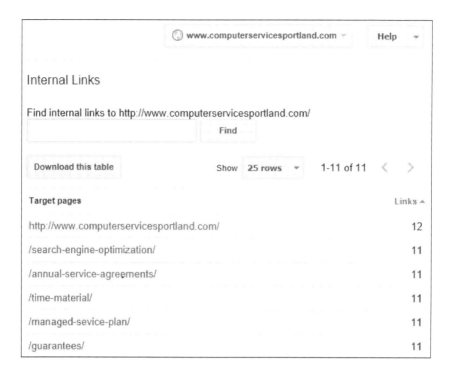

Sitemaps

Sitemaps basically tell Google about the pages on your site so that Google has a comprehensive picture of your site. A XML Sitemap is just a list of the pages on your website. Creating and submitting a Sitemap helps make sure that Google knows about all the pages on your site, including URLs that may not be discoverable by Google's normal crawling process. Hence, this is where you can access all of the information about the sitemaps that Google has been informed of.

A good way to start here is to test a sitemap. To do this simply click the Add/Test Sitemap button, and you will discover if your sitemap is valid. If yours passes the test, then simply add the sitemap by clicking the Add Sitemap button. Please note that the default view here is to only show the sitemaps that you have added. To view those that have been added by other authorized users on the account click the "all" tab. The page shows you the sitemaps that you've submitted, the number of pages they found in each, and the number of those pages that they've indexed. You can also see quite clearly if there are any issues that they've detected within your sitemaps. Simply click on the warnings hyperlink to view them all.

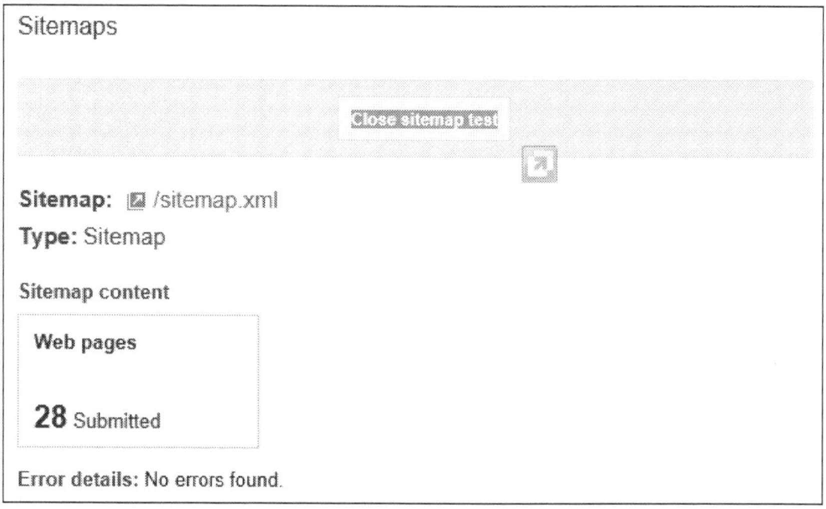

Sitemaps

Close sitemap test

Sitemap: /sitemap.xml
Type: Sitemap

Sitemap content

Web pages

28 Submitted

Error details: No errors found.

Remove URLs

If for some reason you need to remove one of your URLs, then this is where you perform that. The first step is to either remove the page itself or 301 it elsewhere so that it can't be crawled and indexed. This prevents users and crawlers from getting to it, but the URL will still be in the index, and the page can still be found in the cache. That's where this tool comes in handy.

Enter the URL that you want to remove, click continue, then select whether you want it removed from the search results and the cache, just from the cache or if you want an entire directory removed. Clicking Submit Request adds it to the removal queue. Please note that typically this request will be processed in about 2-12 hours.

Structured Data

The Structured Data page lists each type of structured data discovered on your site, along with the number of URLs containing each type. To see source URLs, click an item. In the Source URLs list, click a link to see the structured data Google was able to extract from that page. To see how a piece of structured data might appear in Google's search results, click Rich snippets preview.

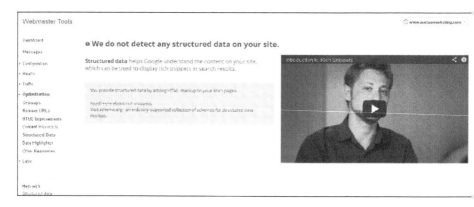

HTML Improvements

This page shows you potential issues Google has found when crawling and indexing your site which are typically with your title and description tags. As titles and descriptions should be unique for each page and should be within certain character length ranges, this section points out where you have issues that can and should be corrected. For example, if all of your tag pages have the same description you're not telling the search engines much about what is on those pages. Clicking through on any of these errors will give you a more descriptive overview of the error and will also give you a list of pages where the error was detected.

HTML Improvements Last updated Feb 11, 2013	
Addressing the following may help your site's user experience and performance.	
Meta description	**Pages**
Duplicate meta descriptions	225
Long meta descriptions	0
Short meta descriptions	5
Title tag	**Pages**
Missing title tags	0
Duplicate title tags	197
Long title tags	0
Short title tags	0
Non-informative title tags	0

Content Keywords

This section displays the most common keywords found by the Google crawler. Please note if you see an unexpected or unrelated keyword(s), that's usually an indication that your site may have been hacked, so definitely visit this section regularly.

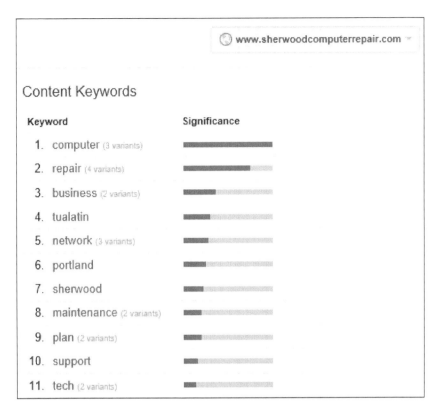

Data Highlighter

Data Highlighter is a webmaster tool for teaching Google about the pattern of event-related data on your website. You simply use Data Highlighter to tag the data fields on your site with a mouse. Then Google can present your data more attractively -- and in new ways -- in search results and in other products such as the Google Knowledge Graph.

For example, if you use Data Highlighter to tag data (name, location, date, and so on) for the events on your site, the next time Google crawls your site the event data will be available for rich snippets on search results pages:

Lupo's Heartbreak Hotel - Things to Do - Providence Journal
thingstodo.providencejournal.com/.../11365-lupos-heartbreak-...
Come to The Providence Journal to get information, events, reviews and ...

Wed, Oct 3	The Punch Brothers
Fri, Oct 5	Wolfgang Gartner
Fri, Oct 12	Waka Flocka Flame

Tagging a page is easy. You don't need to change your site's HTML. Just highlight data items with your mouse and select their type.

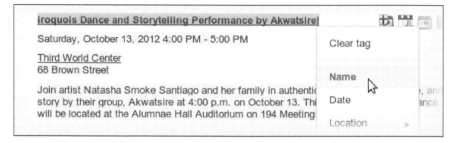

Tag a set of similar pages all at once. Start with one typical page. Data Highlighter will automatically tag similar pages for you and stay in sync with updates to your site.

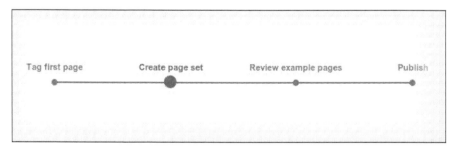

Other Resources

Other resources	
Rich Snippets Testing Tool	Use the Rich Snippets Testing Tool to check that Google can correctly parse your structured data markup and display it in search results.
Google Places	97% of consumers search for local businesses online. Be there when they're looking for you with Google Places for business - a free local platform from Google.
Google Merchant Center	The place to upload your product data to Google and make it available to Google Product Search and other Google services.

This section contains links to tools that are outside of Google's regular list of Webmaster Tools, but are of interest to webmasters, such as the Rich Snippet Testing tool, which enables webmasters to test their schema implementations.

Labs

The labs section contains functionality that's in testing mode. When Google deems that it is ready to be used and incorporated with the other regular tools, then it will be added.

Author Stats

If you want your authorship information to appear in search results for the content you create, you'll need a Google Plus Profile with a good, recognizable headshot as your profile photo. Then, verify authorship of your content by associating it with your profile using either of the methods below. Google doesn't guarantee to show author information in Google Web Search or Google News results.

John Resig - Simple JavaScript Inheritance
ejohn.org/blog/simple-javascript-inheritance/

 by John Resig · in 32,271 Google+ circles · More by John Resig
Mar 20, 2008 – I've been doing a lot of work, lately, with **JavaScript Inheritance** - namely for my work-in-progress JavaScript book - and in doing so have ...

Google News

Nexus 4 sold out in the US? Not quite

ZDNet
7 hours ago Written by
Christopher Dawson

This will just be a quick post since I should get back to real work after trying to buy a Nexus 4 all afternoon. However, it appears that early reports that all US-destined Nexus 4 were sold out were incorrect.

More Technology stories

Custom Search

This allows you to set up Google customized search for your own site. There is a step by step guide that you can follow here.

Instant Previews

This tool allows you to see how your site looks using Google's Instant Preview feature (the view of your site that can be seen in the search results when you mouse over the double arrows that show up next to a result).

Next Step, Add a Local Business Listing To Google Places

First off you need to know where to go. For Google the local business listings are added at the Local Business Center as below at the following address:

http://www.google.com/local/add

If you are already logged in to Google and you have been here before it will list all your current business listings as shown below.

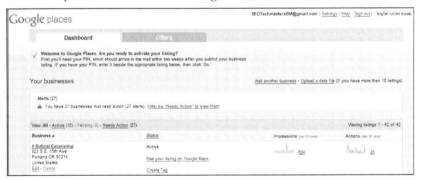

You will notice from screen shot above that there are a few options to configure. Also you see how many times your business was shown on the listings and how many people clicked on it. Only recent information is shown. Notice the option to "View Report" will show you legacy information and give you a more accurate view of the numbers of searches and clicks.

In the next two screen shots you will see how to add the client you saw in the previous screen shot step by step.

This next screen shot shows how you to enter the hours of operation and the payment types that your business accepts.

NOTE: Google has a complete guide to Google Places at:
http://www.google.com/support/places/?hl=en&rd=1

▾ Hours of operations

Make sure your customers know when you're open!

○ I prefer not to specify operating hours.
◉ My operating hours are:

Mon:	9:00 AM ▾	- 5:00 PM ▾	☐ Closed	⇓ Apply to all
Tue:	9:00 AM ▾	- 5:00 PM ▾	☐ Closed	
Wed:	9:00 AM ▾	- 5:00 PM ▾	☐ Closed	
Thu:	9:00 AM ▾	- 5:00 PM ▾	☐ Closed	
Fri:	9:00 AM ▾	- 5:00 PM ▾	☐ Closed	
Sat:			☑ **Closed**	
Sun:			☑ **Closed**	

Are your hours split during a single day, such as 9-11am *and* 7-10pm?
☐ I'd like to enter two sets of hours for a single day.

▾ Payment options

Specify how customers can pay at your business.

☑ Cash	☑ American Express	☐ Visa
☑ Check	☑ Diner's Club	☐ Financing
☐ Traveler's Check	☐ Discover	☐ Google Checkout
☐ Invoice	☑ MasterCard	☑ Paypal

The next screen shows you how to add a logo, picture, and even video describing your business.

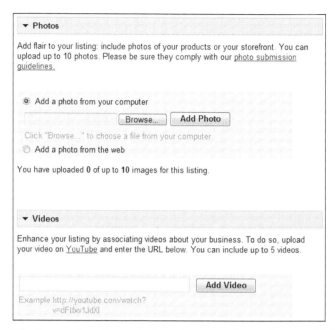

The last option shown below gives you the option to add brands you carry and other details about your business.

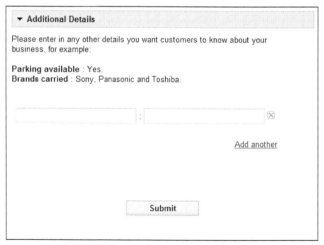

The last screen below sums up all the information you have entered. You will see in the figure my customer's information on Google Local Business Listings which is all the information entered previously.

The last thing we have to do is choose how we want Google to verify our business. Google allows you to either verify the phone number by calling you and giving you a pin number over the phone or you can verify the address by waiting for them to send you a pin number by mail as shown below.

Google Local Business Center

How would you like to validate your listing?
For your protection, we need to verify the information you've just given us. This can be done one of 2 ways:

 By phone
We'll call you at this phone number (503) 692-9082

 By postcard (2-3 weeks)
We'll send you a postcard in the mail to this address

Verifying by phone is the quickest way to verify your listing. To do this you do need to have the phone sitting right next to you because it is less than 10 seconds sometimes before the phone rings to give you your pin number which you need to enter on the main listing screen which lists all the businesses you have listed on the Google Business Listing's as shown below.

A Bobcat Excavating
4590 SW Savannah PL
Beaverton OR 97007
United States
Edit - Delete

Needs Action
⚠ Not yet published ②
Confirmation letter sent Oct 16, 2012.
Enter your PIN: [   ] [Go]
Request another PIN

Create AdWords Express ad

One more really interesting thing you can do in the Google Business Listing's offer and AdWords Express ad. This is basically a link to create an ad quickly in Google AdWords.

> **NOTE:** If you have multiple locations you can add a store code which is a unique ID that you can assign to each of your business locations. A store code must refer to the exact same store across multiple versions of a bulk upload. These codes can help you identify your businesses at a glance.

Examples:

store1, store2
location: NY, locationFL, locationCA
101, 102, 103

The store code must be under 60 characters in length and not contain any leading or trailing whitespace.

Next Step, Adding Your Site To Bing Webmaster Tools

Bing's Webmaster Tools provide some great as well as necessary data for users to assist them with optimizing their website. These tools help you to understand more about your website's traffic, issues with you website, and this tools from a search engine actually provides you with a more comprehensive view of your SEO performance. To get started using these tools you need to first visit the Bing Webmaster Tools page at:

http://www.bing.com/toolbox/webmaster

The first step is to set up your Microsoft account if you don't have one. Just follow the instructions to do this and then you can add your site. Simply enter the URL of your home page and then click on the ADD button. This takes you to a screen to enter a sitemap URL and some basic traffic information about your site.

After clicking the ADD button you'll be taken to the Bing Webmaster's dashboard page where you'll see a thumbnail of your home page. The next step is to verify your site. To do this, click on the "Verify Now" text.

Verification Process

Bing offers three verification methods.

Option 1: Place an XML file on your web server

With this option you'll download a file named "BingSiteAuth.xml" which will automatically have an entry keyed to your account. This file will need to be placed in the root directory of your site. Once it's there you click the Verify button at the bottom of the page.

Option 2: Copy and paste a <meta> tag in your default webpage

With this option you'll take the line of code provided and place it in the <head> section of the home page of your site. Once it's there you click the Verify button at the bottom of the page.

Option 3: Add CNAME record to DNS

This option is more technical than the previous 2, but if you only have access to your hosting solution, and don't have the ability to either modify the head of your home page or to drop files in the root of your domain, then this is the only option that will work for you.

You'll need to add a CNAME record with the name provided to the value verify.bing.com. Please note, there are instructions on how to do this for many well known hosting solutions.

Once this has been done, you just have to click the Verify button at the bottom of the page. If Bing Webmaster Tools is able to verify your site, you will see a green message saying that your domain is verified and your site information will begin to populate over the next couple of days. If you see a red text message stating "We weren't able to verify your site", review the information in the steps above and try again.

Bing Webmaster Dashboard

Clicking on your site takes you to the dashboard. Here you'll see data showing trending data over the last month – clicks, impressions, pages crawled, crawl errors and pages indexed. You'll also see some basic information on your sitemaps, top keywords, and top pages linked to.

Configuring Your Site

Clicking on this tab will give you a dashboard of data for items that you can adjust when configuring your site. For example, clicking on the sub-tabs will give you more detail and let you make changes.

Sitemaps

Here's where you can submit new sitemaps, as well as learn about the success or error status of them.

Submit URLs

If you feel that you have to submit some new content urgently, and you don't believe that you're crawled often enough for it to get into the Bing index as quickly as you want, you can use this feature to submit up to 10 pages per day, 50 per month. Simply enter the URLs, just one per line, and then click the Submit button.

Ignore URL Parameters

On this tab you have the option to tell the Bing crawler (Bingbot) to ignore URL parameters that have no impact upon the content of the page which typically are tracking parameters. The reason that this option is available was because of the concern over duplicate content – same content different URLs. By instructing the crawlers to ignore certain parameters, the idea was that this would reduce the potential for duplicate content. If you are using canonical tags you have no need to use this option as the canonical tags will take care of normalizing your URLs. If you're not using canonical tags, simply enter the key element of the parameter to be ignored and click submit (then get a canonical tag project on your product roadmap so you can ignore this in the future).

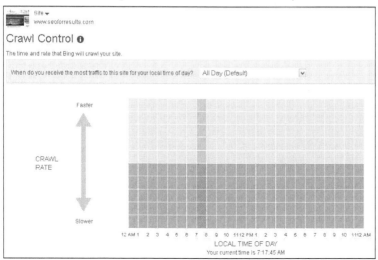

Crawl Control

In this tab you are able to customize when Bing crawls your site for content. Search engines want to get as much good content from your site as possible, so they can provide that content to users to improve their search results, but they also recognize that they don't want to harm your business while they perform this task. Basically, you can adjust when Bing crawls your site for content so they're hitting your site the hardest when your traffic is low and not when your traffic is at its peak. You can choose one of their default options or set the best times for you to be crawled.

Deep Links

Deep Links helps to give your page more visibility in the search results by providing additional content options for users to choose. These are automatically populated based on the pages that Bing feels is most relevant to users. (Please Note- You don't have the ability to add Deep Links, but by clicking on one of the URLs that's been populated you'll be taken to a page that shows the deep links in order. On this page, you have the option to either block one or more of them, and if you choose you can reorder them by rating them via importance.

Block URLs

On this page, you can remove either a page or a directory from the Bing index if you need to. Just select page or directory, enter the URL, and click on either of the block buttons depending on whether you are blocking it from just the cache or completely. (Please Note- Bing doesn't require that you've removed or redirected the original content. Instead, they block it for 90 days, and if after that time period it's crawlable and you have not extended the block, they'll re-index it again.

Disavow Links

On this page, you can inform Bing of any links that you don't want.
Simply select page, directory or domain and enter the URL that houses
the link to your site.

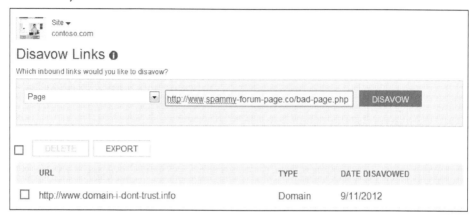

Users

Here you have the ability to add new users without going through the
verification process for each one. Just add a valid LiveID email address,
then select their role (Read only, Read/Modify, or Administrator) and
click ADD. The user you added will then see this site displayed in their
Bing Webmaster Tool's dashboard.

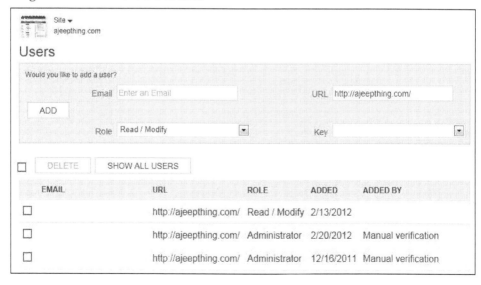

Reports and Data

This section gives you access to reports and data on the effectiveness and performance of your site on Bing. In most of these sections you have the ability just like Google offers to export the data into a spreadsheet.

Page Traffic Report

Page Traffic shows you the traffic stats for the top performing pages on a site. You get to see click data, impression data, CTR Data, the average position when clicked, and the average position when viewed. The View hyperlink at the end opens up a window that shows you the keywords for that URL and their data.

	Site ▾								
	ajeepthing.com								
Page Traffic ❶							Changes for Last 30 days ▾		
						6/27/2012	- 7/27/2012		
Your top pages from organic search							Combined traffic data from [b] [Y]		
EXPORT							See Index Explorer for more details		

PAGE	CLICKS FROM SEARCH	APPEARED IN SEARCH	CLICK-THROUGH RATE	AVG SEARCH CLICK POSITION	AVG SEARCH APPEARANCE POSITION	SEARCH KEYWORDS
http://www.ajeepthing.com/jeep-pictures-1.html	87 ◑	2,446 ◑	3.56 % ◑	3.5 ◑	5.2 ◑	(View)
http://www.ajeepthing.com/stroker-motor.html	190 ◑	2,415 ◑	7.87 % ◑	6.1 ◑	7.5 ◑	(View)
http://www.ajeepthing.com/jeep-models.html	90 ◑	2,296 ◑	3.92 % ◑	3.4 ◑	6.4 ◑	(View)
http://www.ajeepthing.com/jeep-wrangler.html	0 ◑	2,216 ◑	0 % ◑	0.0 ◑	6.2 ◑	(View)
http://www.ajeepthing.com/welding.html	141 ◑	1,796 ◑	7.85 % ◑	3.3 ◑	7.3 ◑	(View)
http://www.ajeepthing.com/jeep-body-tub.html	151 ◑	1,583 ◑	9.54 % ◑	3.9 ◑	6.2 ◑	(View)

Index Explorer

This section provides you with a unique view of how Bing sees your site. It reflects all the URLs Bing has seen on the web, including redirects, broken links, or those blocked by robots.txt, organized in an file explorer-like fashion. This view can help you get some really detailed insights into how your site was seen by the search engine during recent crawls. It can help discover both issues on your site as well as opportunities. A nice feature here is that it shows the sub domains that have been crawled. You can also filter the data to show only pages with 301 redirects, 404 errors or identified malware infections with a single click. Additionally, if you want to see pages that have returned other error codes (i.e., 500 series), then all you have to do is select that range from the HTTP code drop down.

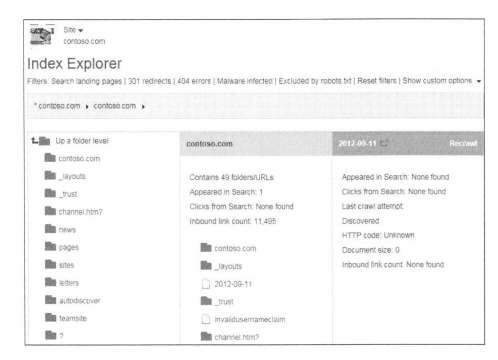

Search Keywords Report

This report shows some analytics and data on your top performing keywords in Bing which come from organic/non-paid search. You'll be able to view the clicks to your site, the impressions, the click through rate (CTR), the average position when clicked, and the average position overall. Clicking on the View hyperlink shows all of the pages that were served up when that keyword was searched.

Search Keywords ❶

Your top keywords from organic search

Combined traffic data from

EXPORT

KEYWORDS	CLICKS FROM SEARCH	APPEARED IN SEARCH	CLICK-THROUGH RATE	AVG SEARCH CLICK POSITION	AVG SEARCH APPEARANCE POSITION	SERVE PAGE
types of welding ▤	9 ◐	394 ◑	2.28 % ◐	3.0 ◐	5.0 ◑	(View
jeep cherokee ▤	7 ◐	377 ◑	1.86 % ◐	7.1 ◐	11.0 ◐	(View
jeep models ▤	14 ◐	337 ◑	4.15 % ◐	5.2 ◑	56 ◐	(View
jeep trailer ▤	16 ◑	274 ◐	5.84 % ◐	7.1 ◐	6.9 ◑	(View

SEO Reports

This is where you get all of the SEO recommendations that will help your site comply with SEO best practices. The SEO Reports provide aggregated counts of all the issues found, across the entire website scanned. Clicking on an item in the SEO Suggestions list takes you to **SEO Analysis Detail** page where the issue is explained and it even shows a sample of pages affected by this non-compliance. Simply click on the error to get a full description of the problem along with a list of the top 50 pages that were non-compliant.

SEO Reports (Beta) ❶

Discover which areas of your site may need work to comply with SEO best practices.

SEO SUGGESTIONS	SEVERITY	ERROR COUNT	PAGES
The <img> tag does not have an ALT attribute defined.	Low	150	109
The page is missing meta language information.	Moderate	109	109
The title is too short or too long.	High	23	23
The <h1> tag is missing.	High	8	8
There are multiple <h1> tags on the page.	High	8	4
The description is missing in the head section of the page.	High	9	9
The description is too long or too short.	High	51	51

Inbound Links

This section shows the external links that Bing has discovered that point to your site. The trending information on the graph displays whether you are increasing or decreasing links. Clicking on any URL, or the number to the right of the URL, will open a popup window which displays the URL that contains the link to your site and shows the anchor text that is used for the link on that page.

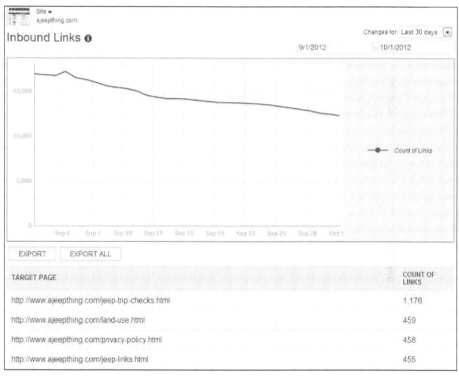

Clicking on any URL, or the number to the right of the URL, will open a popup window which displays the URL that contains the link to your site and shows the anchor text that is used for the link on that page .

Link Details

This table lists up to 20,000 external pages that link to http://www.ajeepthing.com/jeep-trip-checks.html

EXPORT

SOURCE URL	ANCHOR TEXT
http://www.jeep-classifieds.com/16211_cobrand.html	Trip Checks
http://greatamericanroadtrip2010.com/?p=3325	Off Road Checklist
http://www.jeep-classifieds.com/cobrand/willys.asp?s=16211	Trip Checks
http://www.jeep-classifieds.com/cobrand/view.asp?id=32160&s=16211	Trip Checks
http://greatamericanroadtrip2010.com/?p=2911	Off Road Checklist
http://www.jeep-classifieds.com/cobrand/view.asp?id=23752&s=16211	Trip Checks
http://www.jeep-classifieds.com/cobrand/jeepster.asp?s=16211	Trip Checks
http://www.jeep-classifieds.com/cobrand/parts.asp?s=16211&offset=25	Trip Checks

Crawl Information

Here you can view information about crawl issues that Bing has found on your site. This section contains similar data to the Index Explorer section, but provides a different view of the data. To see the pages where errors have been reported, click on the number under the error type.

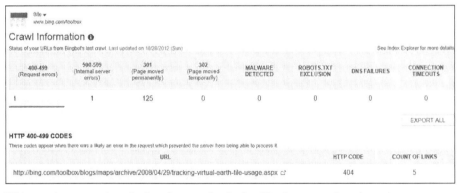

This section contains similar data to the Index Explorer section, but gives a different view into the data. To see the pages that the errors have been reported for, click on the number under the error type and they'll be displayed below.

Diagnostics and Tools

This new section currently has five useful tools that any webmaster can use.

Keyword Research

As is frequently expressed here on SEW, keyword research is one of the fundamental tasks of any SEO campaign. Here Bing gives you access to their keyword research data so you can see the query volumes on Bing for the keywords you're interested in, along with related keywords which can give you ideas for other areas that you may want to target.

Filters

You can select multiple countries in the same language now: for example Canada, the United States, and the United Kingdom combined with English. In addition, you can filter by date ranges (going back up to 6 months) and also filter by language or region. The money icon ($) will display cost-per-click information from Bing Ads when hovered over and provides you with a quick way to buy the keyword. Clicking on a phrase refines the research data round that phrase and reruns the request in the tool. Clicking any column title sorts the data either alphabetically (for keywords) or by number.

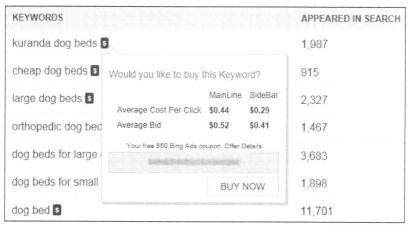

Link Explorer

In this section you can enter any URL and get a list of pages that link to it. This is a great tool to do some competitive and market research since you can use it to learn more about what sites links link to sites similar to yours. There are other filter options available, you can filter by site to get a list of the pages that link to that URL, you can filter by anchor text so you can see who links with "Click Here" and who links with the brand name, and you can filter by the source – internal, external or both.

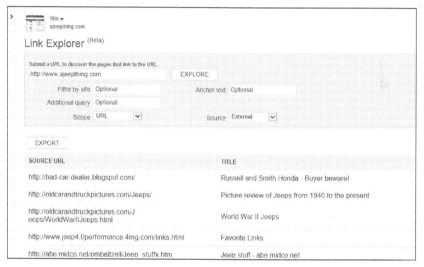

Fetch as Bingbot

If you'd like to see your page as Bing's crawler, Bingbot, sees it, just enter your URL here and click Fetch. You will then see the headers and content for the page displayed. It's a great tool for determining if a page on your site can be crawled.

Markup Validator

The purpose of this tool is to help you understand if you have implemented your selected **structured markup language** in a way which allows Bing to read the information properly for its search results. This tool can be used on any URL to view the special markup applied in the page's source code. The markup languages recognized by this tool are the following: Microformats, RDFa, Open Graph, Schema.org, and HTML Microdata). If the markup has been applied correctly in the code of the scanned page, it will show the markup in a report below the input space.

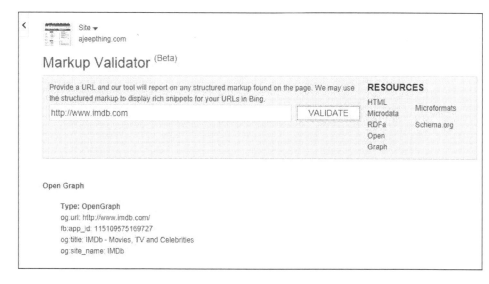

SEO Analyzer

In this section you can receive analysis of an individual page on your site to see what work is required for the page to comply with SEO best practices.

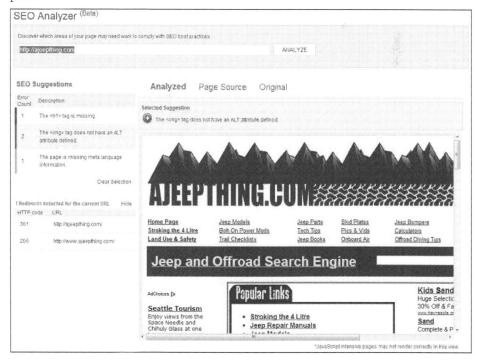

Message Center

This is where Bing will communicate with you in regards to issues from malware detection to crawl speed concerns. You can filter by site if you have multiple ones, and if you have lots of messages you can also filter by message type. It's very intuitive. Further, you can also have Bing email these messages to you. Just click on the Profile link in the top right of the page and check the appropriate boxes to indicate how often you'd like to receive emails, and what types of errors you'd like to be notified about.

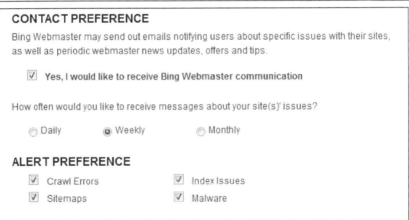

Next Step, Add a Bing Business Portal Listing

First off you need to know where to go. And for Bing local business listings which are now the Bing Business Portal are added at the Local Listing Center as shown below:

http://www.bing.com/businessportal

Here you can add a new listing and create a login. I already have a login, so I will login and immediately it shows my current listings as shown below.

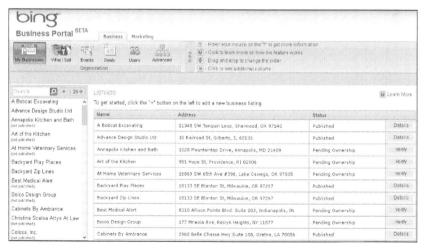

Click on the plus symbol next to the search bar and it allows you to enter a new listing as shown below.

Under more details you can add additional information about the business as well as set the hours and the types of payment you take as seen below.

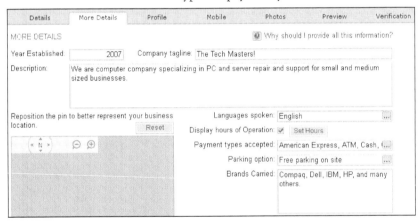

You can set your specialties from a drop down list provided by Bing and also scale the percentage of services or products you provide in the screen below called "Profile".

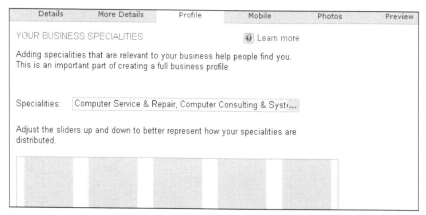

Next you have a unique screen where Bing actually helps you to create a mobile version for your website as shown below.

In the next screen you can set the items you sell and the prices as seen below:

The final screen before the verification process you can upload pictures or logos of your business as seen below.

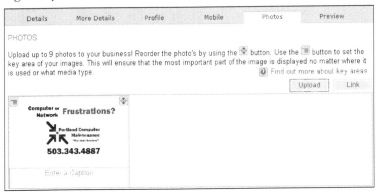

Lastly you have to verify that you are at the phone number or address by selecting the method you want to verify with. Your listing will not run until it is verified.

Next, Add a Business Listing To Yahoo!

Yahoo is still in the top 3 search engines and since Marissa Mayer has taken over it has high hopes this year of making an even better turn around. It still maintains its advertising partnership with Bing.com, so you can bet their share of the search engine market will only grow. Here are the instructions to add your website to the local business listings of Yahoo!. Go to local listing to add your business at the following URL as shown in the figure below:

http://listings.local.yahoo.com/csubmit/index.php

You can also add multiple business types and hit submit to submit your website. There is only one screen to enter information so it is rather simple. When you are done you will see the screen below.

Next Step, Make Sure Your Website Has Good Mechanics

Throughout 2012 Google's algorithm has really taken a strong look at how well a website is designed and coded. So much so that if your website has a high number of broken links, it is almost impossible to get ranked. There are more deal breakers with Google as well such as are your pages too big over 180Kb? Is your website compatible with all the different web browsers including Ipod, IPhone, and Android browsers? How do you find out if you have problems?

Every client I take on gets a SEO Audit by an independent authority. AccuQuality.com Reports provide the most comprehensive reports for the money, however a less expensive report can be obtained from SEOAudits.com. I highly recommend that every website have an audit initially after the design is completed and every year at a minimum. Standards change and their reports keep up. Secondly, if changes you make to the website create broken links or links change to outside websites, they can be effecting your search engine rankings and you will never know it!

If you have ever visited a grading website that looks at your websites homepage in 30 seconds and give you a score, this is not what AccuQuality.com Reports are. These sites provide a basic report and score for only your homepage doing only a dozen or so tests to give your website a grade. AccuQuality.com and SEOAudits.com test every page of your website and each of them do over 400 tests per page. Testing everything from broken links, W3C compliance, browser compatibility, search ability, and much more. They both even spell check your entire website and deliver a huge report online.

Not only do they do a complete comprehensive website report on your entire website, but the report also identifies the line in the code on each page with an issue and instructions on how to correct every issue that the report identifies. For every issue the report identifies, if it is not fixed you lose those imaginary ranking points toward getting ranked well.

Every website I have personally ran with AccuQulaity.com has been found to have over 200+ critical errors identified and many would have never ranked well because of the issues the report identified.

Next, Submit Your Website To Bing

By submitting your website to Bing Business and to the Webmaster Tools you might think...Bing should know I am here right? Well, you want to tell the search engines you are there in hopes they will be quicker to index and rank your website. So don't miss this step because it also tells Yahoo!, MSN, Live, and many other smaller search sites you exist.

To submit your web site to Bing.com, complete the information at the following link:

http://www.bing.com/docs/submit.aspx

Next Step, Submit Your Website to DMOZ

DMOZ (also known as the Open Directory Project), as shown in Figure below as many search engines increase the ranking of your site if they are listed there and rank well. Follow these rules and instructions for submitting your site there:

1. Go to http://www.dmoz.org
2. First find the category that best fits your web site.
3. Choose "Suggest URL" in the top right corner. If it is not available it means that there are more subcategories and you need to drill down and choose the one that best fits your business.
4. Add the Site URL, title and description as shown below. Then select submit at the bottom of the page.

DMOZ has certain rules to follow, as seen on their web site:

- Don't add mirror sites.
- Don't submit an URL that contains only the same or similar content as other sites you may have listed in the directory. Multiple submissions of the same or related sites may result in the exclusion and/or deletion of those and all affiliated sites.
- Don't disguise your submission and submit the same URL more than once.
    Example: http://www.dmoz.org and http://www.dmoz.org/index.html.
- Don't submit any site with an address that redirects to another address.
- Don't submit a site that sells illegal services or products.
- Don't submit sites "under construction."
- Only submit adult or pornographic sites to the appropriate category under Adult.
- You must submit non-English sites to the appropriate category under World.
- Don't submit sites consisting largely of affiliate links.

Violating any of these rules can get your URL removed or not listed at all.

Next Step, Submit Your Website to Alexa

Submitting your web site to Alexa is important as this is another site that helps demonstrate your website's importance to major search engines. To add your web site complete the questions at:

$$http://www.alexa.com/edit$$

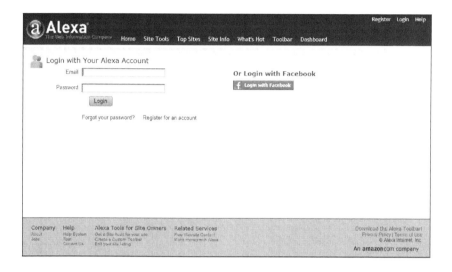

Next step? Use A Major Shortcut! Use Submission Complete to Make the Rest of this Job Easy

There are hundreds of other smaller search engines and services and products directories you need to also submit to. There are also major search engines for other countries. You never know when someone is going to use one of these smaller search engine that might benefit your website. The more places your website can be found the more likely the chance a web user will find your website and buy your products or see the message you are trying to deliver. To have Submission Complete, do all the hard work which might take you weeks on your own go to:

http://www.SubmissionComplete.com

Time is not on your side when you are trying to get a website started or on the right track for SEO. You might have figured out that getting your site included in each search engine and directory is no easy task. There are submission websites which use custom tools that are automated software programs and applications that remember the repetitive information that must be provided in order to get your website listed in hundreds of search engine and directories.

There are also many submission websites that try to scam website owners by promising to submit their site to thousands of search engines and directories for one low fee but just take your money and run. Submission Complete is the only one I use and trust. Every new client I bring on, the first thing I do is use Submission Complete to submit all them all over the web. It would take you months to add your site to every one of these sites on your own. However, for about $19.95 you can have a company that specializes in submitting web sites do it instantly.

Chapter 4 – SEO And Website Structure

This chapter needs to be more about how to apply Schema.org compliance, Rich Snippets, and W3C compliance because applying those principles to your website as these help to improve your ranking. However, this book is about SEO and I would have to create a 500 page book on each of those subjects. So before I delve in to this chapter, I am going to point out that you need to research these items and have SEOAudits.com or AccuQuality.com do an audit on your current website to learn how out of compliance your website really is.

Schema.org Microformats and Markups are definitely a plus for any website. Schema.org was a project launched in June of 2011 with Google, Bing, and Yahoo! collectively. They introduced a reorganization of websites for many reasons but the best part is for Rich Snippets. If you are unfamiliar with Rich Snippets you probably have seen them and didn't even know it. Let's look at an example. Below you see the Trailblazers website at NBA.COM. Underneath you see 4 additional links directly to the rich content. These are Rich Snippets and you configure these using coding for structured data learned at schema.org.

THE OFFICIAL SITE OF THE **PORTLAND TRAIL BLAZERS** - NBA.c...
www.nba.com/blazers/
Official site with news, scores, audio and video files, player statistics, and schedules.
2012-13 blazers schedule - Tickets - Roster - Trailblazers.tv

Google also has Rich Snippets testing tool at :

http://www.google.com/webmasters/tools/richsnippets

The way you design your website may allow you to fall victim to many ranking pitfalls. Google has several new make it or break its where before not doing these just caused you a few ranking points. The most serious of which is bad coding, secondly is not being compatible with the different browsers, smart phones, IPAD and IPods. Another is having more than two broken links on a page. The last is having slow hosting speeds. Google requires a hosting score of 70 or above for good rankings. You can test your website at:

http://pagespeed.googlelabs.com

If your website is written in Wordpress most commercial hosting companies cannot give you speeds well enough to rank well. The reason is Wordpress loads a database, plug-ins, a theme, pictures, and widgets simultaneously.

You need so much more power in hosting than the cheap hosting can provide. Google loves Wordpress more than any other development platform but it loves Wordpress allot more if the hosting speeds are better. If you are hosting a business I highly recommend that you host your website at either of the following:

http://www.WPHostingServices.com

or

http://www.WordPressHosters.com

There are other lesser evils with Google as well though. I often hear similar things from prospective customers when I tell them their old site won't work: "What do you mean? My site looks awesome! It's all flashy and things move here and there. It's awesome!"

One of the most severe is designing your website as a giant picture then adding mappings or building your website in Flash and not having any data to index. You wind up getting a website that Google can't index or find relevant for anything as you can see from the Google Caches snapshot of page below.

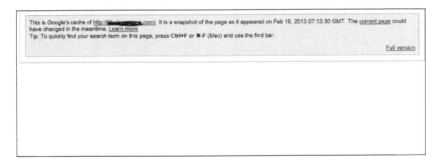

This is Google's cache of http://████████.com/. It is a snapshot of the page as it appeared on Feb 18, 2013 07:13:30 GMT. The current page could have changed in the meantime. Learn more
Tip: To quickly find your search term on this page, press Ctrl+F or ⌘-F (Mac) and use the find bar.

Full version

A website that doesn't use Flash or pictures would be indexed with lots of text as shown on the next page. Search engines cannot look at the text on pictures and index the information. Although Google says it can index some Flash better, for the most part Googlebot can't look at Flash or video either. Not only that but Flash is not compatible with Apple devices.

SEO Management Services

Best Rated SEO Reseller For 2010" – AngelasAndPaulsBacklinks.com

Subscribe to RSS

Subscribe via RSS

- Home
- About Us
- Payments
- Resellers
- SEO on Steroids!

About Us

Old fashion customer service

Web professionals; have come to recognize how difficult it can be for a web developer, programmer, or other online professional to provide affordable, yet quality SEO services to clients.

It seems that a couple of times a month I consult with a company that has a Flash website and loves it to death. It is so tough for them to part with it and sometimes I have to have a overwhelmingly convincing argument and still they ask what I can do to optimize it. The fact is I can do a few things with Meta data and maybe add a secondary website in Wordpress to work alongside their website. If they choose not to listen to my advice and stick with their Flash or picture website I cannot feel bad. The client got what they paid for, competent advice. I am an expensive person and if someone pays me for advice I am going to give it to them. If they choose not to use my advice, I will have no problem taking their money. They got what they paid for.

Also, this is something new that never came up before until this week. If you pay an SEO company to optimize your site during a site redesign, don't change the URLs of the pages that are indexed with the search engines. When a person does find you and the site file names have been changed, when they click on the link to your site, it won't work. There is a process to doing this if you really want to do this using 301 redirects. If you are changing technologies such as from Joomla or ASP to some other technology be it HTML5 or Wordpress, CONSULT AN SEO PROFESSIONAL if you don't want to pretty much disappear from Google completely for a while or lose all the ranking work you have done on your website URLs before the redesign.

Do not trust your webmaster if he tells you that nothing is going to happen. He most likely doesn't know SEO or how search engines work and you will lose your positioning and you will be pretty much gone from Google for sometime if you don't takes steps before you move to the new technology to redirect old links to the new ones. Not just in any, the right way.

SEO or Design Should Be Considered First?

A graphic designer tell you that in a majority of cases the design comes first, of course. Without an aesthetically pleasing design, a visitor will bounce off your site within a matter of seconds. Not so fast. How did they get to your website in the first place? A great-looking website is nothing if there is no one to look at it.

Even if you intend to employ Google Adwords, you will soon realize you are spending a fortune to get visitors. As soon as you stop paying money, you stop getting visits. That is usually when the SEO expert gets called in because of some research someone did to see how to properly market a website without paying Google and Bing their kids inheritance or future retirement.

Then you learn from your poor design and lack of social media, link sharing, etcetera that it will take 6 months or so for the major search engine marketing campaign to try and rescue your website rankings and start getting a scalable number of visitors.

As a business owner you soon learn after soaking tons of money in Pay-Per-Click that you get so much more business cheaper and easier by going the SEO route. So much so that as I mentioned earlier in this book, PPC garners about 11% of all clicks on the Internet. The organic results which are the more trusted results get the other 89% of the clicks. In fact AccuQuality.com's Internet Usage Report in November of 2012 showed that websites utilizing professional SEO services garnered 88% of all clicks on the Internet search engines. This means that between PPC and those using professional SEO, only 1% of search engine directed visits are from websites that don't utilize either of those.

The thousands of business owners that have been through this exact cycle of PPC versus SEO, will certainly argue that PPC is most definitely is not the way you should go, especially when the owners of these sites realized when it was too late. There was too high an amount of profit, potential, and clients lost because the design looked great to humans but was invisible to the search engines and no SEO was utilized.

What is really laughable, though, is that if you actually read the sales pitch on any one of the many of web design companies that own websites, many of them blatantly claim to be SEO experts. You need to watch out because many wear it as if it is a badge of honor or to help them make sales. A quick check of their portfolios soon reveals that if they are search engine marketing experts, then it is clearly evident that their clients are definitely not on the receiving end of any claims they make.

Implementing SEO In The Design Before It Is Live

Many people call me and ask if you can implement site optimization into the design before you launch a website? The answer is absolutely, Yes! The web design and SEO should go hand in hand. The thought process of optimizing a website and creating SEO-friendly website design should form the foundation right from the outset.. Ultimately the content and design will capture free organic search engine traffic and also mark the website as a potential authority on the product or service.

Many times when I take on a website for professional SEO, the cost to optimize or change the website is greater than if we just started from scratch. But it has to be done. I tell family and friends starting a business, have the SEO company design and create your website. That is where a successful business venture starts!

Search engines absolutely do not care about what the site looks like: it is what's behind the scenes that makes the site so much more relevant to them. If we go back to the example a few pages back, my new client's initial chance to make the best impact on the search engine when the site first got indexed was wasted. In contrast, the extra time and money spent on redevelopment for SEO, including the keyword research and SEO copywriting after the initial design was an added expense. It took an extra two months to get it all done and start garnering page positions on Google.

If you want a far better chance of getting good website ranking from day one and even, in some cases, a page-one result faster than you might think start with SEO.

Design And Optimizing For Devices

It is amazing how much traffic is now generated by mobile devices. Just two years ago most website averaged less than 10% traffic from mobile devices. Today it about 35% of all traffic is from mobile devices. These devices include Android, IPHONE'S, IPAD, IPAD Mini's, Car GPS, ONSTAR, and yes even Blackberries, IPODs. My new Tesla Roadster electric car even has a built in mobile device for going to the Internet.

Mainly these devices have all the Internet capabilities of getting on the Internet as a regular PC just with some limitations and a smaller screen. I haven't even seen this addressed in any books yet. Creating a specific mobile website and websites which are compatible with all mobile devices translates in to more sales, more traffic and better rankings.

As a company we have been doing mobile web SEO for larger enterprise companies for quite a while. Just recently has small and medium sized businesses approached us to create a mobile website. Here are some links to help you if you want to do mobile yourself:

- o **Bing Mobile:** http://onmobile.msn.com/en/Products/MobileWeb/BingMobileWeb (Don't forget Bing Business for creating a quick mobile website as we discussed earlier in Chapter 3.)
- o **Google Mobile:** http://www.google.com/mobile/
- o **Google Mobile Sitemaps:** www.google.com/support/webmasters/bin/answer.py?hl=en&answer=34627
- o **Google Mobile View:** www.google.com/gwt/n
- o **Mobile Search Marketing Guide:** www.mobilesearchmarketing.com/guide.php
- o **Technorati Mobile:** http://m.technorati.com

Add your mobile-optimized site to search engines and let retailers know here:

- • **Abphone:** http://www.abphone.com
- • **Bango:** http://www.bango.com (One Click Payments)
- • **Dotmobi:** http://mtld.mobi/sitesubmit
- • **Medio:** http://medio.com/partners/addyourmobilesite/
- • **Mobiseer:** http://www.mobiseer.com
- • **Nokia:** http://www.nokia.com/global

Focus On Your Websites Impact

You should focus on the results you want. These usually include more visitors, leads, customers and sales. Every decision you make should be focused on fulfilling those goals. Keeping that in mind, you might spend a bit less time worrying about the exact shade of blue on the callout background, and more time worrying about things that will improve your marketing results and keep visitors directed toward your goals.

There are countless ways a website design can negatively impact your results. In fact, I would say that more often than not, website designs done without an SEO professional tend to have a negative impact on marketing results.

Another problem occurs when you attempt to implement too many strategies in your SEO. For one, you won't be able to tell which of your strategies are successful and two, search engines don't like it when you lose focus. Most major search engines like to see each of your website landing pages centered around one topic.

Implementing one strategy at a time allows you to determine which strategies are working and which strategies are not. SEO campaigns are most successful when you concentrate on one effort at a time. If you have an existing website you usually have a lot of material that has accumulated over time. These items help your prospects find your website and help you turn them into leads and customers.

When you do a site redesign, make sure you use the same links and file names for your new sites URLs. If you don't, the links that are on search engines will become useless and broken links. The proper way to change the site is to create the new pages with new file names. Use the Robot.txt file to tell search engines not to index the old links. In a few months you can get rid of the old files as they will no longer show on the search engines.

A good general rule is to add new content every day and change the old content as often as possible. The more content you have the more visitors you will have and the longer they will stay. This will in itself grow your business faster. A 100 page website will beat a 10 page website 90% of the time on search engine rankings. A 500 page website is even better. If some of those web pages were written recently, that's even better. But remember, always keep the focus of each page as close as you can to a single topic and optimize that page, the Meta Tags, Title, and keyword density to that topic.

A little known rule that helps add to your imaginary point standings with search engine rankings is that the more often you update your content (while keeping it relevant to your website subject matter), the better.

> **NOTE:** *Blogging makes creating new and updated content easy.*

You want your website design to attract new visitors and increase your conversion rate and the number of leads you get from your website. Over time you should constantly improve the effectiveness of your conversion tools, including your landing pages.

If you build a completely static website and have to go to a web designer, every time you want to set up a new landing page or to change an existing page, you are limiting your ability to quickly experiment and improve on the design. You should have a website that lets you edit content and build landing pages without having to know website code unless you know HTML, PHP, or XML well.

One of the rules you should live by is that you should spend money on resources and relevant content that attracts and converts as well as optimizes your site. You should not overdo a design that limits you to only one type of code, such as websites that include Flash. The code should be dynamic and easy to change. Of course, sometime the easily changed part costs a little more upfront, but not at the end.

If you follow the rules set forth in the last paragraph, you should be able to create ongoing content with a building strategy. When you have more content, you can grow your website. This will help you increase your visitors and grow your business faster.

When you have finished your website, you should constantly have conversion experiments. The key to driving your conversion rate and the number of leads you get from your website over time is to constantly improve the effectiveness of your website. Several sites can be used to test your website:

Website Grader (www.WooRank.com) – Has a useful tool for measuring the marketing effectiveness of your website.

SEO Audits (www.SEOAudits.com) - Can check your website for W3C compliance, browser compatibility, broken links, mechanical errors, SEO issues, and much more.

AccuQuality.com (www.AccuQuality.com) - AccuQuality.com is the best website report you can get on the mechanics of your website and costs more than SEO Audits reports. Although the reports between the two are similar, AccuQuality.com Reports gives more in-depth analysis and actually gives instructions how to fix many compatibility issues with browsers which can help you fix errors. AccuQuality.com reports actually spell check your entire website as well.

The Very Basics Of SEO In Design

We have already hit on the points here, but they fall into this chapter as well. So let's make sure our design or redesign has these points covered:

- Meta and HTML Tags
- Header Tag Content
- Body Text
- Links
- Alternative Tags
- Header Tag Content
- Other Items You Should Make Space For
- RSS Feeds
- Other Valuable Content
- Other Tips

Meta and HTML Tags

Meta tags are HTML tags; they just appear in very specific places on a web page. There are two Meta tags which are given more weight than the others on most search engines. Those are the keyword tag and the description tag.

Most of the Meta tags are also given some weight on less major search engines and directories. However, not all search engines take keyword and description Meta tags into consideration because in the past, these tags have been overloaded with keywords that were irrelevant to the website.

Header Tag Content

This is a simple attribute but about as commonly overlooked by web designers as the Meta tags are. The *header tags* are a bit different from other tags discussed earlier in this book. These are the attributes that set up the different levels of headings and subheadings on your website. There can be as many as six different levels of headings but typically search engines only look at the first four.

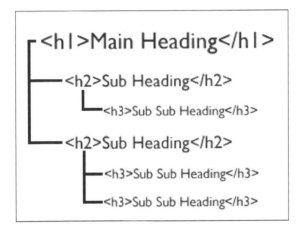

To help you understand this, the title or topic of a web page should be the H1 title that the human side can see. Subheading of the topic should be tagged with the H2 tag and so on–kind of like a tree as above.

So let's say you have a website page that sells motorcycle helmets. The heading hierarchy in this example should look like this:

> H1: (Page Topic) Motorcycle Helmets
> H2: (Main Topic) Buy Motorcycle Helmets and Accessories
> H3: (Sub Topic) Motorcycle Face Shields
> H3: (Sub Topic) Motorcycle Custom Straps
> …and so on.

If there is a new sub topic such as there is in the example, you would start again with an H2 tag.

> H2: (Main Topic)

Headings denote important information and enable users to quickly skim the page to find the information they are seeking. The search engines use this in their scanning of web pages to determine what's vitally important.

Header tags on a web page should contain your most important keywords in a contextually appropriate manner. Specifically, search engine spiders, bots, and crawlers take into consideration the text within a header tags. Looking at the different levels of headings, first-level headings should contain the most important keywords on your web page.

> **NOTE:** *You should use your most important trophy keywords in the level-one heading, then lower-level headings (levels two through six) should contain decreasingly important keywords.*

The heading tags are similar in format to other tags that you've examined to this point and used after the <Body> tag of the website:

> <H1>Header 1</H1>

```
<H2>Header 2</H2>
<H3>Header 3</H3>
<H4>Header 4</H4>
<H5>Header 5</H5>
<H6>Header 6</H6>
```

WARNING: *Search engines are smart enough to know when your keywords are the same shade or color as your back ground and will penalize you for hiding the H1 tags or text that contains your keywords.*

Header tags should be included before the body-text tags of your website, and the text of the header goes in between the opening and closing tags.

Body Text

Like the Header tags, the *Body text* is also text that is visible to human readers of your site. When you look at the pages of this book, for example, the text that is between each of the headings would be the body text – the same way as it is for a web page.

The body text is another place where you want to include your keywords. A good rule of thumb is to use your keywords once in every paragraph as long as it makes sense to a reader.

Sidebar: Keywords in Text

Having your keyword strategically placed in your text on every page is one of the most important elements of any website. Of particular importance are the trophy keywords which we determined in Chapter 2. The trophy keywords need to be placed throughout the text on your primary landing page. It is of particular importance where those keywords appear and how often they appear on the page.

The keywords you choose must match the words and phrases that potential visitors will use when searching for the products or services your website provides.

You can also use additional tags to indicate special formatting in text. Those tags are as follows:

```
<b>Bold</b>
<i>Italics</i>
<strong>Strongly Emphasized</strong>
<em>Emphasis</em>
<li>New Line in List</li>
```

Each of these special tags indicates special formatting for the word or phrase in between the opening and closing tags, and the special emphasis makes a search engine crawler take notice of those words.

> **NOTE:** *You should try to use keywords within the special tags if possible. Only use keywords where appropriate, and avoid stuffing keywords into your site simply to improve your search engine rankings. If you use those tactics, they will most likely fail and may even get your site banned from some of the search engines.*

Sidebar: Things to Avoid

To make your website's body text visible to spiders, bots, and crawlers, avoid the following:

- Text embedded in JavaScript applications or Macromedia Flash files cannot been read.

- Text contained in images such as those with extensions .jpg, .gif, .png, and .bmp cannot be seen.

- Text that is accessible only on a submission form is not readable.

Most of these things make your site look flashy and cool. Site designers struggle with these issues and sometime choose looks over site optimization on purpose to make the site owner happy. There are only about 8 different fonts that can be used on a website without pictures because of the standards. Also, certain text styles cannot be indexed by search engines.

If search engine spiders, bots, and crawlers can't see your website text, then they can't index that content for visitors to find.

Links

You should have an area of your landing page dedicated to links. The links should be related to the content of the page and be active links to real websites. *Broken links* will lower your search engine rankings on major search engines.

Links have always been an important factor in how websites rank on the different major search engines. Most important are not only links from your site but to your site as well, as we discussed in Chapter 6.

Alternative Tags

Alternative tags for pictures and links are also important to have on your pages. These are the tags that are a brief description of a picture or graphic on a website to explain to spiders, bots, and crawlers what is displayed.

These Alt tags are also a good place to include additional keywords to make your site more relevant. Human users will never see your Alt tags unless they intentionally turn off images to enable web pages to load faster.

Other Items You Should Make Space For

Your website should have some of the items below on its main landing pages. The more of these the better. Each one of these increases your site's value on different major search engines.

- A little flash
- Conversion page (submission page)
- RSS Feed
- Video (YouTube if possible. It is owned by Google.)
- Blog (BlogSpot if possible. It is operated by Google.)
- Facebook, MySpace, or Twitter Feed or Widget
- Links to other pages in your body text
- Text links to other pages in your website if you use pictures, maps, or Flash for buttons.
- Text that can change frequently.

Adding RSS Feeds

Really Simple Syndication(RSS) or it's sometimes referred to as Rich Site Summary is an XML-based content format for distributing news, headlines, content, and more about a website. It is almost a requirement now for higher rankings to have an RSS feed on your website or blog to rank well.

RSS Feed readers come in all shapes and sizes these days. The Firefox browser has one built right into the Bookmarks feature. I personally use Google Reader. (http://www.google.com/reader)

You can also create feeds for your own website so your audience can subscribe to them. If you update your content frequently and promote the feed effectively, it can help drive more steady traffic to your website.

Advantages of Creating RSS Feeds

This is an excellent way to bring repeat traffic to your site. Think about it, every time a web surfer opens their RSS reader to get the headlines for all the sites they monitor, they'll also see your site's updates.

Instead of relying on them to bookmark your site and return at a later date, their RSS reader keeps your site fresh in their minds.

Many entities are now pushing out their newsletters and switching to this method of content distribution because you don't have to worry about dodging the spam filters.

When you send an email newsletter more than half of those people won't even receive it due to spam filters or junk mail algorithms. With RSS feeds, you don't have to worry about that because you're not sending an email, your simply sending out a news feed for all the readers to pick up.

How to Create an RSS Feed for a Static Website

If you are novice in creating XML code, I recommend using www.feedforall.com for static websites. They have an easy-to-use feed builder that lets you create and manage all your feeds in one place.

Once you have created your feed you have to upload the XML file to your web server. FeedForAll.com will automatically convert your feed into the XML format so you don't need to worry about additional formatting or coding and make your RSS Feed URL something like:

http://www.yoursite.com/yourfeed.xml

Anytime you add a new article to your feed, that XML file is updated.

FeedForAll also has a built-in upload feature so you can upload the XML file right to your web server with their software, as long as your web host has FTP access.

Creating An RSS Feed From a Blog

Google allows you to create an RSS feed using their blog website Blogger.com. WordPress is another website type that offers a free blog equipped with RSS feeds.

Other Valuable Content

Other Items that can be considered great content:

- A free whitepaper
- A how-to or manual
- A series of articles
- A YouTube video
- A podcast
- A badge or image
- A proprietary study
- A quiz, poll, or test
- A joke or cartoon

- A calculator or free software
- A blog or forum
- A wiki or knowledge base

Other Website Considerations

For a website to rank well, the search engines must retrieve information from the website – not so much from the human side but from the coding side. The retrieval of data is a combination of the activity from the crawler, spider, bots, the database, and the search algorithm used by each search engine. These three elements work together to retrieve web pages that are related to the word or phrase that a user enters into the search engine's user interface.

The algorithms change frequently, which is one reason this book is updated every year. In SEO, ranking is what you'll spend the most time and effort trying to change. Your ranking in a search engine determines how often people see your page.

How search engines rank a page or pages is a difficult science to figure out and changes frequently. Search engines don't want everyone to know the exact science. If it were known to everyone it would be tough to get on the first or second page of a search.

Ranking is such a large part in search engine optimization and appears frequently throughout book. There are some things that can give your website an advantage right from the beginning. Let us take a look at two: hosting location and frequency of keyword use.

Hosting Location

There are a lot of locations that we talk about in this book. In this section of the book, I will specifically refer to the location where you host your website. I have a customer who is in good straights now but had tried to handle his own optimization. No matter what he did he couldn't get his website off of page 68 on a Google search. At SEO For Results, we do a complete SEO Report to find issues with the website. What we found was that the website was being hosted on the same server as several porn-related websites. In SEO terms we call this being in a "Bad Neighborhood." That is where porn or blacklisted websites are using the same IP or IP Range as your website.

In this case, the website owner had bought his hosting on eBay for $42.00 per year. If you have a respectable business website, you have to be hosted on a respectable hosting provider. The Major search engines do not like to rank websites that contain pornography, racial comments, or other such content.

Keyword Frequency

Websites must be relevant to the keywords you choose. So the frequency with which the keywords appear on a web page may also affect how a page is ranked in search results for that keyword. For example, on a page about office furniture, one that uses the words "office furniture" five times might be ranked higher than one that uses the words only two or three times.

When word frequency became a well-known factor, some website designers began using hidden words hundreds of times on pages, trying to artificially boost their rankings. Almost every search engine recognizes this as *keyword spamming* and ignore or even blacklist pages that use this technique.

Tips

- Don't repeat keywords in your title tags. Repetition can occasionally come across as spam when a crawler is examining your site, so avoid that in your title if possible, and never duplicate words just to gain a spider, bot, or crawler's attention.
- Include a call to action in your title. There is an adage that goes something like, "You'll never sell a thing if you don't ask for the sale." That's true on the Web as well. If you want your users to do something, you have to ask them. The title is never a bad place to ask. But include your trophy keywords there, too.
- Create a website that contains Meta tags, content, graphics, and keywords that help improve your site ranking.
- Use keywords liberally on your site, so they are used in the correct context of your site topic and content. Keep them relevant and search engines will keep you relevant.
- Include reciprocal links to your site from others as long as those links are legitimate and relevant to the topic of your website.
- Continuously encourage website traffic through many venues, including keyword advertising, reciprocal links, and marketing campaigns.
- Submit your website to search engines manually, rather than wait for them to pick up your site in the natural course of cataloging websites.

Keyword Density

One of the biggest design rules to keep is the number of times you use your keywords (known as *keyword density*). Most search engines allow a relatively low keyword density. Google is by far one of the less lenient in this regard when ranking websites. Google likes to see a keyword density of 5 to 7 percent – much lower and you risk one of your competitors outdoing you in the optimization area or much higher than that and you risk your website bring penalized. Bing, Yahoo!, MSN, and other search engines seem to be stricter and want keyword densities of about 5 percent.

Use a word processing program to find out your total word count. Paste the HTML source code of the page into a blank document, then choose File, Properties, Statistics, Word Count. In Microsoft Office 2007/2010/2013 it is found at File, Prepare, Properties, Statistics.

There is also a great tool to use to see the number of words and the keyword density on a page. http://www.gorank.com/analyzer.php. This tool is the most accurate.

Let's move on. If you are optimizing that page for a single keyword, you need to figure out how many times that particular word is repeated within that 250 word total.

Manually scan the page and count every repetition of your keyword. If you have Microsoft Word 2007/2010/2013, you should also have an Replace function under the Home tab all the way to the right. Paste in the code and then type in the keywords in both the edit box and the replace box. The program will replace each occurrence of the word with itself...and produce a total count for the number of repeats.

Let us assume for this exercise that you have used a keyword 10 times on your page. To calculate the keyword density - take that figure and divide it by the total number of words on your page. So in this case 10 divided by 250 = .04

Keyword density is always referred to as a percentage of the total word count for the page. So now you need to multiply .04 by 100 to get the percentage figure.

Your calculation would look like this;

.04 x 100 = 4%

The page has a keyword density of 4%.

For effective optimizing that will boost your pages into the Top 20 spots on the major search engines you are aiming for a keyword density of between 5-7%.

What you have just been shown is about as simple as it gets for working out the keyword density of a web page. To recap, the formula looks like this:

10 divided by 250 = .04 x 100 = 4% -or- keyword count divided by total word count x 100 = keyword density in percent. So you can add your keyword another few times without penalty on most major search engines.

Algorithms fluctuate constantly at the major search engines so it is much simpler to optimize a few pages for different weighting or densities. A few pages at 5%, 6%, and 7% keyword density will mean at least one of your pages should rank well on each major search engine.

Chapter 5 – Off-Page SEO

If you are on page 1 of a Google search for the keyword or keywords that relate to your website you get all the business. Of course divided by the other 9 websites on page 1. If you are on page 3 or later, you are in a virtual black hole. As I mentioned before, good SEO is about 30% what you do on page. Meaning how your website is designed and the content on your website.

Now let's look at the other 70% which is what makes your website appear to be authority on your websites subject matter. This includes everything from where your website is listed, reviews you get, how many visits you get, how much social media mentions your domain name, and the number of links from other authorities on the Internet to your website.

All of these things must appear natural to Google and the other search engines or your website will be just a memory. That seems like a lot, but let me break it down for you in the next few sections:

Placing Keywords In Your Incoming Links

The anchor text used to link to the web page should contain important keywords or keyword phrases. The linking text is viewed as "contextual" by search engines especially Google but can't be the same on a large number of incoming links thanks to Google's Pengui update.

The Google PageRank is based on Larry Page's, a co-founder of Google, idea that a website that has good content and is more important will be linked to by many others. This is one reason that incoming and reciprocal links to your site are given a very high importance to its search engine rank.

Incoming links are links on other websites to your website. This metric is more reliable in search engines' eyes, because it is much harder to manipulate another person's website. If a link appears on the CNN home page, linking to your website with the term 'great travel website' in the anchor text, search engines can see that a highly respected site believes your website is worth linking to for the topic "Travel Websites". When it sees this it acts as if there is an imaginary voting system on the Internet and the link from CNN counted as a vote.

The Quantity Of Incoming Links

Link building is one of the biggest SEO tasks. You can get your website to a Google PageRank of 2 without a single link, but after that your site needs to become relevant to the search engine with as many links as possible from sites that are in the same industry, related social media, other websites related to your websites topic or are news organizations.

Search Engines will often monitor the quantity of incoming links to a website. A large quantity of incoming links is an indicator of popularity or importance, and the search engines will favor sites with a larger number of what are now as backlinks. Search engines use the volume of incoming links to give better ranking to the more popular sites.

However, there is plenty of places here to get in trouble. If you go and create 10,000 links in a week and then no other links are ever made, you are likely to get blacklisted from Google. Link building needs to have an appearance that it was made naturally and gradually.

If you are in marketing there is something I hate to tell you. Most consumer don't like you. In fact consumers are tired of your advertising on TV ads, billboards, and full page newspaper ads. They literally complain and rebel against pop-ups and pop-under ads, CPM, CPA, and CPC ads. They see ads now in bathrooms, on their phones, and especially the internet. I have seen a growing movement of people deliberately going out of their way to avoid advertising or complaining to any listening ear about them.

As an SEO person, I am in the marketing business, in virtually every aspect of social media. I consider myself an expert at creating links, building content, making links, and creating a web presence for my clients without them realizing they are being advertised to or it is in the interest of SEO. Because as soon as an online visitor gets a whiff that what you're doing serves a marketing purpose, it doesn't matter what the quality of the content is they will duck for cover, and go away.

It is time to educate you on not only what is SPAM but how to avoid becoming a spammer yourself. First I will tell you how to get the best type of links. The ones that come from official news sources.

Incoming Link Quality

Not all links are created equal; therefore some link builders will spend months trying to get one strong link from a big, important, or relevant website. A sometimes good link-building tactic is to try to get thousands of links from smaller sites, which are presumably easier to get than a link on a highly prestigious site. Many of those websites will not stay low ranking and build up a ranking of their own. When they do you reap an even greater benefit.

Once you realize the importance of relevant incoming links to the success of your website, you will understand the need to engage in link building and how a professional ongoing link building campaign is paramount to the success of your website.

There is a reason that search engines care about links to and from your website. Remember our imaginary point system from the early chapters? The search engines treat your incoming links from other relevant websites as a "point" for your site. The more you have the better. Some sites give you more points. News outlets such as LocalNewsDay.com, TheKnowVegas.com, ChicagolandNewspaper.com and CNN.com help your rankings increase faster because Google sees them as an official news source. A single link from a positive news story can be the equivalent of getting 300 PageRank 3 links from websites. That is from a single link. That is how important Google feels the links from official news sources is. Other site types that seem to give more points are .EDU and .Gov websites that provide links to your website.

Bad Links

The number of pitfalls to link building are limitless. You have to be very exact when it comes to following the Google Webmaster Guidelines. If you see advertisements for the following type of links....Think twice.

- **10,000 links for $29.95 –** Very dubious offers from spam emails offering you 5000 links for $19 are too good to be true. They lead almost directly to a penalty.
- **Paid links on high PR sites –** It's actually quite easy to get noticed when you buy links on so-called high PR sites where the toolbar PageRank is 6 and above. When one website gets in trouble for buying links from the same sources, everyone listed gets the same penalty by default.

- **Hidden links in WordPress themes or counters –** Some Word Press themes sites are just SEO scams which rely on hidden links in the themes to be spread around. If you rely on such links for "link building". You will eventually be penalized. Some visitor counters have done that in the past as well.
- **Artificial link profile -** with always matching anchor text – when every single link to your site is well optimized saying something like "SEO company" this might look too artificial to stay unnoticed by Google.
- **Wrong language links –** Its obvious to search engines that an English site having thousands of links from Russia, India, Pakistan, or China makes the website standout and open to penalizing or blacklisting. Google engineers are smart enough to compare the language of your site and the sites that link to you.
- **Gaining too many links too fast –** it's not always the more links the better. Even good links gained too fast can result in a penalty. Link building must be natural. If you get 10,000 links in a week, you better be prepared to do that every week forever or Google will see it as unnatural.

Official News Sources

I am going to give away one of my best kept secrets. For years I have had access to over 50 official news sources that have been able to give me the best links to my clients websites and deliver a marketing message to my clients they could not get anywhere else. Not only does the news articles deliver the marketing message you want to deliver, it doesn't appear to be an advertisement, you create trust in your product or service, and you get a link back to your website that is the equivalent of hundreds of medium quality links.

So how do you do get the best link in the world for less than $50.00? Take a look at below. You will notice that the main article is about coffee fundraising and then there are ads under sponsors. Both of these great ways of getting links back to your website from official news websites that Google has determined are official news sources. There are many local news outlets nationwide. They have online newspapers as well as small paper newspapers you can get at supermarkets and local businesses. They like educational articles and they love to help those that are advertisers. It is a perfect example of, "You scratch my back and I scratch yours."

There are some rules though. First you usually need to pay for a banner ad for the website. Usually less than $50 per month. It is about $30 per month for TheKnowLA.com which has about 15,000 visitors per week to their inline news site. TheKnow news franchise has local newspapers in major cities all over the country and an add will run about $40 per month on each website. One of the most expensive is Chicagoland Newspaper which runs about $75.00 per week but they have almost 20,000 unique visitors per day.

After you purchase advertising you need to submit a news article that is of journalistic quality where it doesn't seem like an advertisement. One that interests people but doesn't mention your company name until late in the article where your company and website are mentioned as an expert in your field and a quote from someone who is an expert in your company.

This way you educate the consumer, give trust in your company, get a link to your website and deliver your message without appearing to be an advertisement. This is one of the best ways to subtly advertise and get your message to the consumer and your help SEO at the same time and at a very low cost.

So who do you talk to do this? Here are my personal list of contacts.

Contact	Online News Source	Email Address
Mike Smith	TheKnow Franchise	MikeSmith@TheKnowLA.com
Ty Nguyen	Chicagoland Newspaper	Ty@ChicagolandNewspaper.com
Chris Sales	NYC News Desk	Chris@NYCNewsDesk.com

Good Website Links

There are an infinite number of places you can get good links to your website that are relevant and will increase your rankings. These are:

1. Websites in your industry (Experts, your suppliers, wholesalers, industry regulators, Industry training and certification sites.)
2. AngelasAndPaulsBacklinks.com is a monthly inexpensive newsletter with hundreds of easily obtainable links, articles on how to obtain links, and places that offer free homepage and deep links.
3. Charity websites, educational institutions, places you sponsor
4. Chambers of commerce, BBB, Industry associations
5. Customer reviews
6. Old sites with established domains
7. News organizations
8. Press release sites
9. Blogs and forums
10. Buy a blog instead of buying links on a blog.
11. Quality news articles
12. Websites from .gov and .edu sites
13. Social media and bookmarking sites
14. Customer review websites
15. Anyplace that you feel will bring you positive and relevant branding to enhance your company's credibility.

Sidebar: Getting Good Links From Customer Reviews

Google's acquisition of Zagat and its use of Yelp's customer reviews brings a great way of creating links back to your website and at the same time increase social mentions of your website on the web.

If you break it down, there are four types of businesses on the web:

- Businesses that get most of their business from referrals could care less about reviews.

- Businesses that get most of their business from referrals, get online reviews and think that nobody reads them or even cares about them.

- Businesses that think reviews are important and work hard to get a s many as possible.

- Businesses that try to get reviews and don't get very many.

The types that rely heavily on referrals and ignore reviews don't realize that some time in the next year or two someone is going to write something about them online and there is a very good chance it's going to be negative. Your website can avoid some of these by providing a way for people to give comments on your website. Whether public or not and always make sure you follow up on comments that are negative.

If negative comments get around on the Internet, which it usually does thanks to Google, their referrals are at risk of drying up. If the first thing that shows up in Google for your brand name or the your websites domain name is a negative comment or review, you are potentially in a very bad spot and risk losing business. In some extreme cases I have seen a company go out of business.

Positive reviews are great, the real power is in the reviewer. A customer willing to spend the time to review you is a brand ambassador is always a powerful ally. Instead of just asking them for reviews, you should be thinking about how you can harness your relationship with these valuable people to help spread the word, both online and off.

For those of you that try but can't seem to get any traction with reviews, you should consider the following, on how to build review generation into their business processes.

Customer Review Acquisition Strategies

When you get right down to it, there are basically four ways to get an online customer review:

1. Via phone

2. Via email

3. Via a Website

4. Via transcription from a hand-written reviews

Which method is right for you depends on how you conduct your business.

One of the biggest mistakes I see is businesses that don't collect email addresses for advertising. Most of the businesses I work with know they should but rarely do. Even when they do, they don't keep their list up to date and one clients list we worked on recently had less than 10% with current addresses.

If email doesn't work for your company, then you'll need to consider how you typically interact with your customers. If most of your business is done in person then give them a comment card to complete and then put those comments online. If it's over the phone, you may have to do it via mail. Try stapling a comment card with return postage to your invoice. Especially for those clients you have gone out of your way for.

When figuring out your customer review acquisition strategy, ask yourself what your staff can realistically do every day.

Some tips for asking customer reviews:

1. Offer Incentives? A large percentage of your customers will do it for free. If you offer to pay your top clients, it's possible it will backfire and they will get turned off, which could hurt your business by dampening the enthusiasm of these clients.

2. Make it easy for customers, but don't send them a link to review you on Google unless they have a Gmail address.

3. Do not ask people for Yelp reviews. This almost always backfires. You may get a few positive reviews in the short term, but if your customers are not active Yelpers, Yelp's SPAM filters remove them. You'll end up with no reviews and potentially some angry customers who wonder why their hard work reviewing your company went away.

4. Send a request to review your company promptly. Don't wait. People are most likely to give you feedback right away when they are happy with your service or product. The longer you go from the time of service to the time of your request, the higher the likelihood your customer will not give you a review.

5. If you have the customer's email address, follow up your initial request three days later with a reminder email containing links of where to go for review submissions. Reminder emails can account for a huge percentage of review conversions.

6. Don't setup a kiosk in your business. Funny thing is that some companies allow people to login to their Gmail and leave a comment right there in the business. The problem is, that all the reviews come from the same IP address. Even though they are valid, most SPAM filters and Google will see that they came from the same IP address and think they are being spammed.

Tip: I have often heard from business owners they feel embarrassed when asking customers for reviews. If that sounds like you, my advice is to be totally candid with your customers. In other words, under promise and over deliver and hope for good reviews. One good way is to tell your clients that you are working on improving your business and online reviews are a good way to do this. I have found that this kind of candidness makes the asker feel better about asking for reviews, which improves the chances of actually getting them.

If you still can't figure out the review thing there are several companies out there that would be glad to help you such as the following:

- AngiesList.com
- CustomerLobby.com
- CustomerRating.com
- DemandForce
- MoreBiz.com
- Ratepoint
- Yelp

Link Juice

The term "link juice," refers to the voting power that a link passes to a page in which it links. The fact is only Google knows exactly how much link juice is getting passed on from each link on a page. However, there are some basic factors we can use to determine how valuable a given link will be. Look for links with these qualities for better results:

- The page is relevant to your content.

- The link from the page to your page has a good anchor text.

- The other outgoing links on the page look relevant and appear to be to quality sites.

- The text around the link that you will receive is relevant. The page has been recently cached by Google, within the month. To check the cached date please see the instructions in Chapter 1.

- The page is a respected or authority page such as a charity, news, educational or government website.

Sidebar: The Orphan Page Link Test

An orphan page is a page that has no links from any other page and hence cannot be found by search engines. If you want to test if Google learns links. Place a link to the orphan page.

The next time Google indexes your page with the link to the orphan page, check to see if the orphan page was indexed by the search engines. If your orphan page gets indexed by Google, then there is a good chance the page you are testing is passing on link juice.

Linking Within Your site

It's easy to focus only on inbound links, but there are important best practices for linking within your site as well:

Site maps – Create a good one. If not for your visitors, for search engines. It's rough for search engines to have to drill down and find all that content. Make it easy for them. Oh, and keep it updated! Secondly you need to make sure that you have a site map for the search engines. Preferably an XML site map which you list the location in your Robots.txt file as well as upload it to Google Webmaster Tools.

Anchor text within content – This may be even more important for onsite links than for offsite links. You have full control of your anchor text, so use it. Plus your site theme is already in place, so each link will have complete, natural relevance to the page it points to.

Breadcrumbs – Are a little piece of search engine love. Breadcrumbs are not only helpful for navigation, but search engines can pick up great anchor text from them. Breadcrumbs are the navigation elements that large sites use to help categorize content, and allow you to find your way back to core categories if you lose your way.

Featured products, news, etc. – Links from your homepage are, in general, considered more important than links from other parts of your site. So if you've got something you really want to show off, it makes sense to put it on your homepage, not only for usability, but for search engines as well.

Links to yourself – Link to your product or service pages from your own blogs, articles, resource sections, news releases, or any other relevant pages. Use the anchor text within each of these resources to send a little link love to your core pages. So, for example, if you sell toothbrushes, and you write a blog post about correct brushing practices, link the word .toothbrushes" from your blog post to your main toothbrush product page.

Ways Of Creating Great Content

Here are some great ways you can spend money to add unique content and value to your site:

1. Write how-to guide.
2. Place your brochure on your website.
3. Build microsites which are websites that focus on a single keyword or topic and work best when the keyword is in the domain name.
4. Build better keyword density landing pages.
5. Create a buying guide or catalog for your most popular product categories.

6. Write weekly press releases and news articles.
7. Create video reviews of your products or services.
8. Write open letters to your customers.
9. Care — deeply — about the quality of your writing, and about your audience.
10. Go deep with original research.
11. Share a never-before-seen interview.
12. Avoid redundant, duplicated, or stolen content.
13. Build so much trust with your audience that people would be happy to hand over their credit card.
14. Build your authority — and your site's authority.
15. Spell correctly.
16. Fix factual errors.
17. Don't use bad grammar or text language
18. Write for humans to read but be acutely aware of search engine bots.
19. Create something nobody has ever seen before.
20. Remain balanced and worthy of your audience's trust. Don't take one side over the other. You chance making a majority of the people upset.
21. Cover a topic comprehensively.
22. Create something people would want to share and bookmark.
23. Don't overuse promoting promotions, calls-to-action, and ads.
24. Write something a good magazine or journal would print.
25. Spend an a lot of time on detail.
26. Create something people want to talk about positively.

Other Things On Your Linking To Do List

Look at all the free links you have pointing to your website. Also use Google Webmaster Tools and an SEOAudits.com Report or an AccuQuality.com Report to get familiar with its 404 and 302 reports, log files, broken links, . Make sure that your own links and those pointing to inactive URLs, and URLs that are going through multiple redirects. Make sure all links are finding their ways to your active pages without passing through 302 redirects or some sort of redirect chain.

In my line of work, every time I beginning a new SEO campaign for a client, it never ceases to amaze me how many broken links I find in on their website. On some bigger websites there are thousands of broken links, not only from the website but to the website. The ones coming to the website to pages that no longer exist. If you used 301 redirects to fix these issues you would get the link value of those incoming links. These are free links that you earned! Make sure they are 301 redirected to active URLs.

Buy A Blog

Buy a blog instead of buying links is what I tell people. Google literally loves WordPress more than anything especially when you host it at a different IP as your website and get discussions going. Buying a blog can be a much more effective use of your money in the long run as well. You'll get a lot more value than just the links, and you will never run the risks of being penalized for buying paid links

Using Social Bookmarking Sites

To get your links on social bookmarking sites, all you have to do is create a profile and post them. That part is pretty easy. Getting people to bookmark or vote for your links can be the tricky part.

To get people to bookmark or vote for your links, you need to be patient, and you need to be active on your chosen bookmarking site(s). Find other people with similar interests and colleagues that you already know. Share their links. They will be more likely to pay attention to and vote for your links in turn.

Popular bookmarking sites include:

- del.icio.us - The oldest social bookmarking website and most popular. Users can also add people to their networks and share bookmarks.

- StumbleUpon.com – Has a browser add-on for saving and sharing websites. Works with IE, and Mozilla.

- Digg.com - Digg allows you to submit stories, then digg users can "Digg" the stories, and make comments. Users can also upload videos, images and podcasts.

- Sphinn.com - Social bookmarking site for marketers. Allows you to share news, articles, etc., and participate in discussions

Using Directory Links

Search engines have not abolished directories. Google has simply gotten much stricter when it comes to acknowledging specific directories. Despite that, they are still beneficial for building page ranking and increasing traffic.

There are many different types of directories that can be of great value to your website or blog. You can search for directories on Google for good ones or for a small fee you can get your website submitted to thousands of directories by having services such as SubmissionComplete.com or WebsiteSubmitter.org do the work for you. These sites charge between $15 and $69 to perform the submissions. But it sure saves a lot of time.

Buying Text Links Is A "No No!"

This is definitely an example of what not to do as we mentioned in Chapter 1 talking about the Google Penguin updates and Panda updates. The major search engines do what they can to make sure a website's popularity is not increased by the use of paid links or link farm. The cheapest link buying comes from Russia, India, Pakistan, Nigeria, and the Philippians. Google know where links are created and that is the fastest way now to get a red flag.

Creating Outgoing links

Outgoing linking is critical for blogs and websites. Many webmasters stopped linking out in order to hoard their PageRank from others in their industry but now it backfires. Having too many outgoing links can be as bad a having none. Somewhere between 15-70 outgoing links on your homepage can be healthy for a website. But this invites a lot of challenges. You need to make sure that your links going out to other websites remain valid (Not broken), they don't link to those in a bad neighborhood (porn, spammy, hate, or political sites, etc.), there are no hidden links and they generally are in the same or a related industry, local, association, or a link to a website Google might consider a possible vendor.

Where are my links from?

There are several tools that can let you see what links are targeting your website. I was saddened that Yahoo Site Explorer went away in 2012. There is only one other I highly recommend and that is Majestic SEO (http://www.majesticseo.com). Google also has a limited link report now included in their Google Webmaster Tools console but it only gives output on what they find relevant and I have seen their relevant links reporting to be less than 1% on some websites.

Diversity Of Your Links

When trying to gain links you need to get a diverse number of quality links. If all the links you are building are from Blog postings with a PageRank of 1 it is very easy for Google to detect since that is very unnatural. You want to get links from sites with different PageRanks an not just blog postings.

It is best to choose a range of sites that are big, small, popular, unpopular, no PR, higher PR, etc. You should never ignore potential links from social media sites like Twitter and Facebook or from organizations you get business materials from or associations your company belongs to.

Negative SEO

As if business owners didn't have enough to worry about when it came to marketing their business online when up pops a very real risk of unscrupulous competitors attacking your website in a bid to get your site banned from Google or have your search engine rankings drastically demoted to the lost regions of Google's search results.

There is a bad side to SEO and you can fall in to the Negative SEO trap if you don't watch out for it. This has been an issue for a while, but it is now hitting the mainstream and is now also a tactic your competition may use against you. The harsh reality is that negative SEO practices can cause your site to drop in ranking and even be removed from Google altogether.

A short time ago a business owner bragged about how the more he upset his clients and they complained online about him, the better his ranking results got. Google has since put measures in place to deter website owners from using tactics that are intended to manipulate their search engine rankings using bad publicity.

As a result of negative SEO, practitioners have looked at sites that have been banned as a result of bad publicity, and off-page SEO tactics that have drained websites of their ranking. They then learn what techniques to use to target a website that they want to eradicate or demote. They then use these techniques to harm the competition.

Good SEO companies employ Reputation Management as a early warning system that these issues are happening. It also catches when clients or former employees begin a campaign against the company to harm the website or companies reputation online. There are many techniques that can be used to eliminate or reduce the negative effects that these kinds of comments or linking can do to you if caught early enough. Both for the end user and to the search engines.

Several people who work in the SEO industry have consulted with me on a regular basis when their clients website is under attack from bad commenting, reviews, or other negative SEO practices. Almost every strategy someone can use to demote your website there is a counter strategy to employ to reverse or minimize its effects. In some industries where there is severe competition and we know it is going to happen we employ techniques in advance.

In some cases you know who is doing it. A impossible to please client, a former disgruntled employee, and sometimes it is a current employee who is mad at the company. Other times it is impossible to find out who is carrying out a negative SEO attack because many of the people they have done their research or involved a highly skilled person to help.

This could be another book I write, but if bad Yelp reviews are killing you, you get listed on Rip Off Report, Scammers, etc. It is best that you contact me immediately before your business suffers and it is too late to take any action. The sooner you start taking action to reverse this situation the better.

Google or Bing Link Penalties

When you receive a penalty notice from Google, you are instructed to clean up your act and remove any links that may be violating Google's guidelines. Sometimes you have no knowledge of who placed the links and if there is no way to remove them. Luckily you can keep them from hurting by using the Google Disavow Link Tool in Google or Bing's Webmaster Tools.

Link Spamming

To the all knowing eye, spammy links are easily found. A good SEO company provides links that have the appearance of being an organic and customer or vendor provided link.

Even before social media links had been part of the major search engine's algorithms, they were there, usually from SEO wannabes that didn't know any better. Let me warn you now, if you are involved in social media solely for the SEO value of the links from your favorite social media sites – you're doing it wrong and you are going to eventually meet with a less than favorable outcome.

You are treading in an area where far too many people have already abused this area. So much so that now increasingly savvy community members are *over*-sensitive to it. I have seen legitimate content called SEO spam simply because the user couldn't find another marketing purpose to apply a name to it.

How can you avoid being called a spammer? Provide GREAT, not just good, content that doesn't look like your directly advertising the service or product wherever possible. In general, the better your content = the less likely it will be considered spam. Let's take a look at different types of spammy content:

- Comment Spam
- Blog Spam
- Viral Marketing
- Being The Self Promoter
- Money Making Spam

Comment Spam

This type of spam needs no description. Comment spam is a major annoyance and made entirely too easy with the advent of Deamon software that auto spams. Blogs, Forums, WordPress websites, Facebook pages, social media bookmarking sites, and the like all have to deal with this kind of spam.

When you go to a website, drop a comment with a link back to your website either by hand, use software, or use a bot that drops a link back to you website you are an offender.

You should never comment unless you have something to add to the conversation. Use links only if it is relevant to the conversation.

Blog Spam

Blog spam is essentially when an unknown blog takes high quality content, like a viral video or images, from elsewhere and hosts it on their blog to attract traffic and attention with content they didn't create.

A secondary term called LinkJacking is essentially the same thing, only this time, it is well known/high traffic blogs doing it in order to get traffic specifically from social media sites such as Digg or Reddit.

Another difference between blog spamming and Linkjacking is that blog spamming takes multiple pieces of content from various sources to attempt to hide the fact that it is copied and it really spam. Linkjacking usually takes content from a single source and simply adds a unique description so as not to be "duplicate" content.

Blog spamming serves little purpose but to rob the original content producers of credit for their time and effort in creating the content.

Viral Marketing

Viral marketing is like hitting a "home run" in social media marketing. Having a piece of content go viral gives a number of obvious marketing benefits, especially everyone's favorite marketing buzz word: branding. That's why many big brands try to go this route. The problem? It's becoming harder and harder to achieve. Why? Because it has been done...a LOT. Not only are users becoming more cautious of this type of marketing, but the content's becoming redundant.

How to avoid this label: Your content must be or look completely genuine, stir up *real* emotions, and strive for originality. It's easier said than done, but not impossible.

Self Promoter

There's nothing wrong with the occasional self promotion here and there. The problem is when your website content is only self promotion with little other content or educational purpose. Consumers know when you are being self promoting and not offering to their conversations and it becomes a reason to exit from your online content. When sharing links from your site or blog exclusively and from nowhere else, people consider this spamming. Even if it's super fantastic, neat-o content, you're spamming people. Even if your blog has no advertising, marketing or business model: you're still a spammer.

When you share more than your own product or service, URL, etc., Not only are you better received, but others will be more willing to share your content again because they trust what comes from you. Sharing nothing but your own content, is the easiest way to end up in a place like Reddit and reported as a Spammer.

http://www.reddit.com/r/reportthespammers.

Reddit.com is a place people can go to report the good and bad about websites. Now, we have all heard the phrase, "the squeaky wheel gets the grease," well the same concept applies right here. More people come to reddit.com to report spammers then they come to remark on how well someone is doing.

Money Making Spam

Most social media users feel if you get paid to submit links to Digg or Reddit, you are a spammer, even if the site(s) you've submitted make no money from it. If a site has too many ads, too large a call-to-action, or even too prominent a brand message, it might be considered spam. Even well known publications have been known to fall victim to this label. The fact is, if someone has something to gain by content being spread then it probably smells of marketing. And if it smells of marketing, than it probably is marketing.

You should limit your call-to-action advertising or comments. If you can, you should always hide your main business objective and first focus on making sure your content is being spread and educational if possible.

Varied Linking Text

Just to give a little history, once webmasters figured out that links helped your rankings, all sorts of abuse started to occur. People started creating ways to beat the system including link farms, massive reciprocal link networks, automatically generated content with automatic links, and automated software that automatically posted to thousands of links on the Internet. Most of these links were never meant for a human visitor to see.

This is where the major search engines began to fight back. They didn't want junk in their results any more than searchers wanted to see it. Search engines started counting some links more than others, and discounting some links and types of links entirely. Then they started to ban websites for using these practices.

Now, link building is no longer a simple "more equals better" formula and the mathematics behind search results has gotten much more complicated. Meanwhile, the ability to use "right link building" has actually gotten a lot easier.

Vary the anchor text slightly for your links allows your linking to appear natural to the search engines. The text used to link to a webpage should be varied and if possible contain a positive word. So if your keyword is " Dentist", you might put "Great Sacramento dentist" or "Best Sacramento Dentist" as the anchor text for your keywords.

Sidebar: Getting Good Links

Anchor text is the visible, clickable text of a hyperlink (also known as link text). For example, if this were a website, then in this sentence, this would be the anchor text. You don't always have control over your anchor text. If someone links to you from their blog, or someone writes an article about you, the writer may not give you "keyword friendly" anchor text. In those cases, just be happy they linked to you. But, in other cases, you may be able to choose your anchor text.

Search engines pay particular attention to the anchor text that they are following. So, for your anchor text, use descriptive keywords and anchor text variants under which you would like to rank and make sure the keyword you are using in your anchor text is linked to a page on your website focused on the same keyword. Many people make the mistake of making every link to their homepage. This gives your homepage a good ranking but all the other pages on the website suffer.

> **TIP:** Pick up the phone and make a call to the administrators/editors for the website you want a link from. Such a simple concept, and one that's adopted by virtually every sales organization in the world, and yet the vast majority of link builders out there fail to utilize the phone, instead opting for mountains of emails or heaps of social network messaging.

WordPress Blog Commenting

When commenting on blogs, particularly WordPress blogs, use a keyword phrase in the "name" box and use a 4 to 5% keyword density when commenting on the blogs. That will often result in a backlink to your website for which you have control of the anchor text.

Forum Posting

When posting in forums, include your keywords or phrases as part of your forum signature as well as writing with your keyword in mind at a 4-5% keyword density is another way of encouraging backlinks.

Chapter 6 - Google Analytics

Google Analytics provides great data and information for you to learn more about the performance of your website. For example, you can learn more about how much traffic your site is attaining, when the busiest time during the day is for your site, where your traffic is coming from and much more. Further, you can sync your Ad Words to Google Analytics to gain greater insight about your marketing campaigns.

To create your own Google Analytics account go to:

http://analytics.google.com

Fill in the required information and you will soon be on your way as shown below

Home

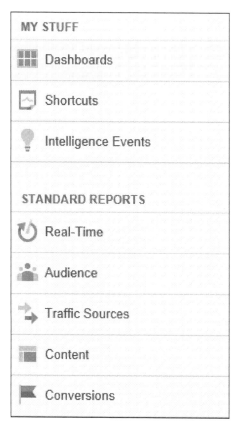

This section is very basic as it simply just displays the URLs that you have set up for Google Analytics. All you have to do to get to the reports is click on your URL links and you will be taken to your dashboard.

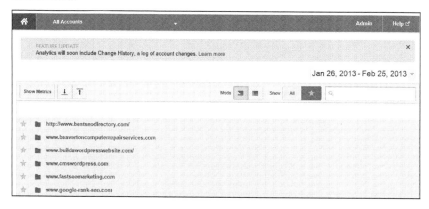

Dashboard

This screen will provide you with some select reports to give you a quick snapshot of how your site is performing. Initially, your dashboard is pre-populated with some basic reports, but you can customize the reports that are displayed on your dashboard to get the data that you want. Each report that displays various metrics is known as a widget. Please note that you can create up to 20 dashboards, and each dashboard can contain up to 12 widgets. You can also email your dashboard reports as well as download them into PDF's.

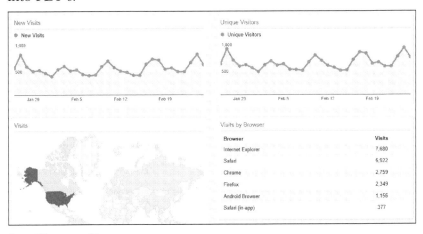

Intelligence Events

In this section Google will notify when your site experiences big spikes in traffic or large drops, and these episodes or events are known as Intelligence Events. Google bases these events off of your site's traffic history. There are two types of events that occur here: automatic alerts and custom ones. Automatic Alerts are generated by Google via their statistical data, and when an event occurs such as a large spike in traffic or a large drop, this is where you will find out.

	Metric	Segment	Period	Date	Change	Importance ↓	
1	Avg. Visit Duration	Country / Territory: United States, Region: North Carolina	Weekly	Jan 20, 2013 - Jan 26, 2013	145%		Details
2	Avg. Visit Duration	Keyword: zip lines	Weekly	Jan 27, 2013 - Feb 2, 2013	222%		Details
3	Avg. Visit Duration	Country / Territory: United States, Region: California	Daily	Feb 1, 2013	>500%		Details
4	Avg. Visit Duration	Source: (direct)	Daily	Feb 1, 2013	>500%		Details
5	Avg. Visit Duration	Campaign: Backyard Zip Lines	Daily	Jan 28, 2013	133%		Details
6	Avg. Visit Duration	Medium: PPC	Daily	Jan 28, 2013	133%		Details
7	Avg. Visit Duration	Source: Bing/Yahoo	Daily	Jan 28, 2013	133%		Details
8	Avg. Visit Duration	Country / Territory: United States, Region: California	Weekly	Jan 27, 2013 - Feb 2, 2013	150%		Details
9	Avg. Visit Duration	Country / Territory: United States, Region: Virginia	Weekly	Jan 20, 2013 - Jan 26, 2013	63%		Details
10	Avg. Visit Duration	Country / Territory: United States, Region: New York	Daily	Feb 17, 2013	223%		Details

A Custom Report is created by you so that you can keep close tabs on the data that is most important to you. For example, you can set an alert if your site experiences a 25% increase in traffic or if your revenue falls 10%. You can adjust the settings so that Google will either email or text you when this occurs so that you can respond immediately. These Intelligence Reports can be viewed in four ways: the Overview, Daily Events, Weekly Events and Monthly Events.

The Overview gives you a snapshot of your automatic alerts and your custom alerts for a specified date range. Daily Events display automatic and custom alerts per day for the specified date range. Weekly Events display automatic and custom alerts per week for the specified date range. And Monthly Events provide you with automatic and custom alerts per month for the specified date range.

> **Tip** - The Find Reports & More feature allows you to quickly search for reports that are offered in Google Analytics and it also shows you your recently viewed reports. So if you are looking at a report and then you get distracted for a bit and can't remember which report you were viewing, then this tool will be handy.

Standard Reporting Options

Real-Time

Real time analytics allows you to attain data about your site's traffic and performance as it happens live. The data will appear within seconds of visitors hitting your site and the data will be displayed in

141

units of time for the last 30 minutes (ie. The past 30 seconds, the past 60 seconds, 5 minute increments and live).

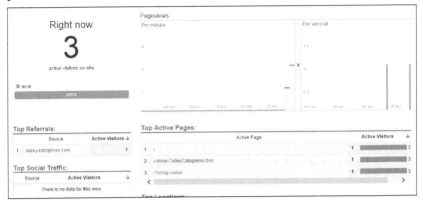

Some of the data you can attain is the number of people on your site at the current moment, the visitors' geographic location, the sources that referred them to your site and which pages they are viewing. Marketers and website owners can use this real time data to gain insight if for example perhaps they have changed or testing some new content on their site and are running a one day promotion.

The four reports that are displayed on the screen above in Real-Time are the Overview, Locations, Traffic Sources and Content. Please note that the Overview screen also shows your top Social sites that have brought you your traffic and the top keywords.

Audience

This section provides some accurate data and info about your visitors. The three main areas of insight that can be gathered here are: where your audience is coming from (geography), how they are reaching your website (eg. via a mobile device or some other device and even what browser they are using), and their behavior on your site which indicates how interested they are in your site.

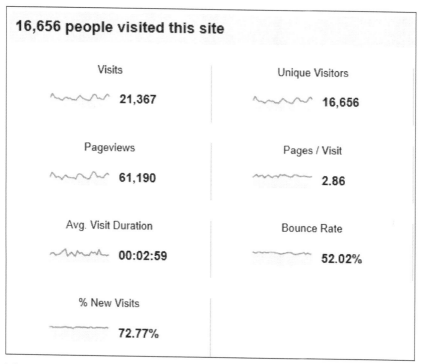

The Overview tab will provide a nice snapshot of the aforementioned reports and then you can drill into the other tabs for this tool to look deeper into the data.

Demographics

Under the Demographics tab you can learn about the exact geographic location (city & country) and language of your audience. This data is great for marketers because it lets you know where your audience is mostly coming from, but it also sheds some light on where some potential new markets may be.

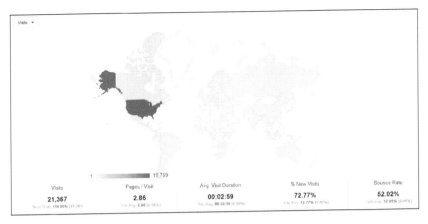

Visits	Pages / Visit	Avg. Visit Duration	% New Visits	Bounce Rate
21,367	**2.86**	**00:02:59**	**72.77%**	**52.02%**

Behavior

Under the Behavior tab, you can learn about the number of new visitors vs returning ones (and the percentage), the frequency of these visitors and how engaged they are.

The new visitors vs. returning visitors report shown above gives you great details about how many pages on your site each of these audience groupings views per visit and how long they stay on your site. You can also attain the revenue value (ecommerce) of each of these audience subsets.

Technology

In this section you can get information about what browser shown below and operating system (OS) your visitors are using to view your site. This information is valuable for not only you but also your IT department if you have one.

Browser	Visits ↓
1. Internet Explorer	7,680
2. Safari	6,922
3. Chrome	2,759
4. Firefox	2,349
5. Android Browser	1,156
6. Safari (in-app)	377
7. IE with Chrome Frame	73
8. Mozilla Compatible Agent	34
9. Opera	13
10. Mozilla	2

This report also provides information about which service provider (ISP) your audience is using to access your site. Knowing which service provider your audience is utilizing to access your site, allows you to figure out their connection speed so that you can determine how technologically advanced you can make your site.

Service Provider	Visits ↓	Pages / Visit
1. comcast cable communications inc.	1,827	2.91
2. road runner holdco llc	1,741	2.96
3. at&t internet services	1,235	2.79
4. verizon online llc	1,215	2.87
5. cellco partnership dba verizon wireless	903	2.45
6. service provider corporation	857	2.12
7. charter communications	743	2.97
8. comcast cable communications holdings inc	642	3.19

For example, if the service providers offer the fastest connections then you can offer your audience top quality videos and dynamic graphics. This is also useful info to know because if your site is very high-tech but your audience is connecting via an ISP that offers a subpar connection speed, then your site's performance will suffer.

Mobile

This report gives you insight into your audience's behavior on your site and what mobile devices they are using to view your site. This information is very useful for your business owners who might be wondering if they should make the expenditure for a mobile version of their site.

For example, even though you might have a small percentage of traffic that comes via mobile devices, this traffic source might be responsible for a large portion of your revenue. Please note that if you utilize mobile apps then you can track and attain insight about your traffic here. It is recommended that you set up an ID for each app to keep it simple.

Content

This report shows visitor activity by custom segments that you create yourself by modifying your Analytics tracking code.

Page		Pageviews	% Pageviews
1. /?crtag=value		12,195	19.93%
2. /-strse-Zip-Line-Kits/Categories.bok		6,005	9.81%
3. /		4,583	7.49%
4. /-strse-37/Ultimate-Torpedo-Zip-Line/Detail.bok		3,192	5.22%
5. /-strse-Trolleys/Categories.bok		2,822	4.61%
6. /-strse-Seats-&-Harnesses/Categories.bok		2,676	4.37%
7. /-strse-Zip-Line-Accessories/Categories.bok		2,601	4.25%
8. /-strse-Cable/Categories.bok		2,584	4.22%
9. /Install-Tips.html		1,782	2.91%
10. /-strse-Installation-Tools/Categories.bok		1,714	2.80%

This tracking information is useful for ecommerce businesses because you can adjust the settings to find out the number of times a visitor has say placed an item in their shopping cart and then removed it.

Visitors Flow

This reporting tool provides accurate insight into the trail your audience takes when they go through your site. Visitors Flow will let you know where this traffic is coming from, the pages they look at, and which page they exit from.

Note that each column represents a page on your site and the step by step route that each visitor took while visiting your site for the time period that you select. You can even set the controls to view the traffic that comes from tablets and via mobile.

Traffic Sources

Similar to the other overview reports, this one gives website owners an overview of traffic source metrics for your site.

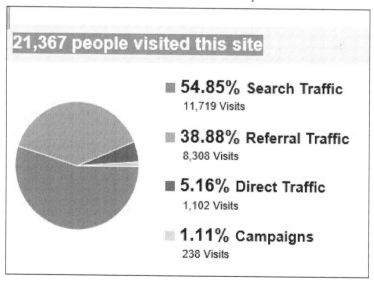

The graph displays the daily number of visits to your site and the pie chart provides you with the percentages of traffic by source type (Search, Referral, Direct). Below the pie chart you can click on each of these types of traffic sources to attain deeper insight.

Sources

In this report users can attain detailed metrics on the traffic that they receive directly to their site when a user types in their URL or visits via a saved bookmark, and they can get info about their referral traffic which is when a user clicks a link to your site from another source (website, social media, an email, video, etc.)

	Source / Medium	Visits ↓	Pages / Visit	Avg. Visit Duration
☐	1. google / cpc	8,186	1.81	00:02:09
☐	2. backyardziplines.com / referral	7,639	4.63	00:03:56
☐	3. google / organic	1,480	1.76	00:02:18
☐	4. (direct) / (none)	1,102	2.04	00:04:29
☐	5. yahoo / organic	1,098	2.09	00:02:50
☐	6. bing / organic	909	1.99	00:02:29
☐	7. stores.backyardziplines.com / referral	347	2.54	00:03:24
☐	8. Bing/Yahoo / PPC	238	1.76	00:02:51
☐	9. google.com / referral	26	1.69	00:01:25

These two reports will let you know how much brand identity or recognition you have in your market via the direct report and which sites are driving the most referral traffic to you.

Search

This tab gives you an overview of some metrics about the percentage of your traffic that is organic and or paid (via ads). Under both the organic and paid tabs you can learn more about which of your keywords are performing well and boosting your results.

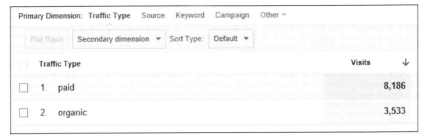

Hence, if this report shows some keywords that are performing well for you that you are not utilizing as much as others on your site, then you had better adjust your strategy. Further, this report also gives some insight into which search engine is sending you the most visitors. AdWords users will want to check this report often.

Campaigns

Under this section in the Traffic Sources, a user can attain metrics on the performance of their AdWords campaigns. Here you will be able to view how effective your campaigns are and if you are getting your desired results as well as if you need to adjust your strategy. Remember the key to getting better results and better at this in general is testing your campaigns and measuring the results, refining your strategy and doing it again…and again.

Search Engine Optimization

In this section you can attain data about your website's search history and results. In order to get this data you must have added your site and verified it with Google Webmaster Tools and configured SEO reporting in Google Analytics.

The SEO Metrics that Google uses:

1. **Impressions**—the number of times any URL from your site appeared in search results viewed by a user, not including paid AdWords search impressions

2. **Clicks**—the number of clicks on your website URLs from a Google Search results page, not including clicks on paid AdWords search results

3. **Average Position**—the average ranking of your website URLs for the query or queries. For example, if your site's URL appeared at position 3 for one query and position 7 for another query, the average position would be 5 ((3+7)/2).

4. **CTR**—clickthrough rate, calculated as Clicks / Impressions * 100

Queries

This report shows the Google search queries that generated the most impressions, the number of clicks, and click throughs to your site. It also displays the average position of your URLs from these Google queries. As we are all vying for that #1 spot from a Google search, this data will help you understand what are actually the top keywords that are driving traffic to your site.

Landing Pages

This report simply displays your websites top landing pages from Google search results. Again this is great data for you so that you can understand where perhaps your site is performing well and subpar. If most of your traffic is coming from organic searches, then knowing your top performing landing page provides you with knowledge of where you should devote more of your efforts.

Geographical Summary

This report gives you a detailed account of which countries the clicks, click through's and impressions are coming from. If you select Google Property via the Primary Dimension, you can see the source of this search traffic (web, mobile, image, video).

Social

Social Overview

This section gives you a snapshot of visitors that find their way to your site via social sources. It also provides you with a conversion value for the goals that you set up. If a visitor to your site via a social channel immediately converts on their initial visit then this will be shown under the Last Interaction Social Conversions. If this visitor just visits, but comes back later to convert, then this action will be shown under the Assisted Social Conversions.

Network Referrals

This report gives you a quick understanding of how much of your overall traffic is coming from social channels. You can also view which networks and the direct links that are driving this traffic.

Landing Pages

Here you can clearly see which of your pages are receiving the most visitors from social channels. If you click on the actual URLs it will show you the actual social source. So if you are creating a lot of content on various social channels, you can learn which of these channels is your top performer.

Conversions

Here you can see the total number of conversions as well as their value that have come via a social source. You can also see the statistics on how many of these conversions were from Last Interactions versus Assisted Social.

Plug Ins

This report allows you to see which articles on your site have been shared via a social button and the number of times. Please note that this report will automatically give you Google+ data, but for Facebook and other data you need to modify your tracking code. Insert this link to learn more about this operation:

https://developers.google.com/analytics/devguides/collection/gajs/gaTrackingSocial

Visitors Flow

This report provides a visual map which helps you to understand what social channels your traffic is coming from and where that traffic flows or moves once they visit your site. Hence you can learn what pages your visitors visit and even where they drop off or depart your site. Once again this report is very helpful so that you can understand which social channel drives your traffic and what pages on your site attain the most traffic.

Cost Analysis

At the time of this edition this report is in Beta mode which is Google's way of rolling out new reports before they become part of the standard set. This report allows you to get a handle on the cost of your campaigns versus the revenue which shows you your margins. Metrics can be show for your AdWords campaigns as long as you have linked your AdWords and Analytics accounts, and even your non-Google campaigns (you just have to upload the data). Once you have your paid marketing channels connected to Analytics you can get your ROI (return on investment), margins and RPC (revenue per click) for each campaign you are running.

Advertising

AdWords

Campaigns

This report gives you detailed data on the behavior of the visitors to your site such as: the number of visitors, the number of pages per visit, the average duration of each visit, the percentage of visitors that are new vs returning, the bounce rate and revenue results (if your site is selling products). Obviously, this report is very useful to learn which of your campaigns is driving the most traffic to your site and you can discern which of your campaigns might need some adjusting. For example, if you see that one of your campaigns is driving lots of visitors to a landing page but your bounce rate is high, then you should most likely take a closer look at the layout and content of that landing page.

Keywords

This report gives you a snapshot of the traffic as well as revenue that is driven from each of your keywords. Here you can get an idea of which of your keywords is performing the best and the most efficient.

Matched Search Queries

This report is fantastic because it shows you how closely aligned your keywords are to what your audience is searching for. Hence, this report is going to show how efficient and valuable your keywords truly are. If you have an ecommerce site, then this report will be very useful because it will provide you with detailed data on how your keywords are performing and how they are impacting your revenue.

Matched Search Queries

24.33% of total visits

	AUDIENCE
▼ ADVERTISING	
AdWords	^
Campaigns	
Keywords	
Matched Search Queries	

Explorer

Site Usage	Goal Set 1	Goal Set 2	Ecommerce

Visits	Pages/Visit	Avg. Time on Site
● **10,615**	**5.54**	**00:02:53**
% of Total: 24.33% (43,626)	Site Avg: 3.81 (45.51%)	Site Avg: 00:02:11 (32.10%)

ing: **Matched Search Query** Match Type Other ▼

①

Secondary dimension: Keyword ▼   Sort Type: Default ▼   🔍 advance

Truth!   **Lies!**

Matched Search Query	Keyword ⊗	Visits ↓	Avg. Time on Site	Bounce Rate	Goal Completions	Revenu
calico critters house	calico critters sale	2,184	00:02:57	35.30%	74	$3,644
calico critters camper	calico kritters	945	00:03:45	32.80%	21	$1,609
little critters toys	calico critters toys	550	00:02:54	37.45%	15	$884
calico critters deluxe village house	calico critters deluxe	155	00:02:15	47.10%	4	$3
calico critters cloverleaf manor	calico critters toys	148	00:01:33	46.62%	2	$558
calico critters townhome	calico critters houses	143	00:04:24	30.77%	4	$327

② (near "little critters toys" row)
③ (near "46.62%" cell)

Day Parts

This report helps you to refine the timing of your campaigns because you can learn what time of the day and which day(s) of the week are the most optimal for your ads. You can see each of your campaigns by the hour for each day of the week to evaluate their performance. You can even attain useful data on your keywords to see when the best time for each one is.

Destination URLs

This report is fairly straightforward as it lets you see how each landing page is performing from your campaigns. Hence you can see how much traffic is hitting each page, their behavior and if the end result you want is happening.

Placements

This report allows you to view where on Google's network your ads are displaying. For example, if you are displaying ads on Google's managed and automatic networks, then you can see which is more efficient for your brand. Additionally, you can gain insight on the actual URLs where your ads are appearing to learn if you might need to adjust your ads to improve their performance.

Keyword Positions

This report gives you information on where your ads actually appear on Google's search results (i.e. right column or at the top with other ads) and the traffic that derives from these ads. Hence, if your ads are not appearing perhaps where you desire them to be, then you might want to up your bids to gain those coveted spots on Google's top page.

Chapter 7-Social Media

Let's go back to my analogy in the early chapters where everything you do adds to the imaginary points value that Google and other major search engines use to assess your rankings. The more you make your website interactive, the longer people will stay. The general thinking is, the more *social media elements* you add, the more often visitors will visit and find your website relevant to its subject matter.

Search engines believe those rules mentioned in the last paragraph, so you should make social media play a big role in your website's optimization. If you are a novice you might be asking right now, "what are social media elements?" When you understand what social media elements are, it's not a long leap from there to *social-media optimization.*

Social media is content created by people using highly accessible and scalable publishing technologies. A better definition might be that social media elements are works of user-created video, audio, text or other multimedia that are published and shared in a social environment, such as a blog, wiki, or video hosting website. Well known sites that engage in social media are Google Plus, BlogSpot, Pinterest, Houzz, Reddit, Twitter, YouTube, LinkedIn, and Facebook. You shouldn't discount the need to engage review websites which also act as product and services directories like Angieslist.com, Yelp, City Search, or Customer Lobby.

Creating your own social media elements such as blogs on your website or participating in other social media websites is what brings traffic to your website and adds to your websites content. One of the best things about social media is that in general most elements are free in terms of monetary investment. There is, for the most part, no cost to participate in these networks except for your investment of time, which depending on how involved you get could become substantial.

When correctly tapped into social media, marketing spreads like a virus. This is why it is sometimes called viral marketing Viral marketing is a not a bad thing. When you participate in social-media, you can almost guarantee that your marketing will soon have that viral quality you're seeking.

Unfortunately, social-media optimization is not as simple as going to a website and signing up or starting a one paragraph blog and waiting for people to come to your website. For the most part, they won't.

Approaching social media in that manner will waste your time, and by the time you figure it out the bad reputation you may leave behind may haunt your website or domain name. Managing your reputation on the web is called *reputation management* in SEO circles and I could write another book just on this topic. I have hundreds of stories on what to look out for and stories of companies ruined on the web because of social media.

The basics to keep yourself from having a bad reputation in social networking is this: when you provide input using social media methods, make sure you do the following:

1. Provide only relative content and no exaggerated claims.
2. Add positive comments and don't make it appear as though you are trying to outdo someone else or are advertising your services. People don't forget when a faker tries to jump in their midst for purely marketing purposes. You are marketing but this is social networking. You are making friends.
3. If you are an expert, make sure your claims are accurate. There are real experts on every subject who will point out your flaws with actual data.
4. Don't ignore people's issues with your product or service. Address them immediately or you are inviting everyone who has ever had a small issue with your product or service to add their two cents.
5. Don't bad mouth a competitor – your only inviting a tidal wave of retribution from your competitor and others.

Seems easy enough, right? Social-media optimization is about first joining communities and creating relationships or friends. It's by going through the process of becoming part of the community and providing relevant and helpful information that your brand will begin to be recognized by other community members. That's when you can announce that your website has useful information, and your efforts will begin to pay off.

Social Media's Value

Some sites have obvious value in social media. Websites such as Google Plus, Twitter, YouTube, and Facebook are all websites that no one thought would amount to anything when they began, but they each suddenly took off in their own way, becoming some of the most popular sites on the internet.

Internet users like something to do and to be a part of something bigger. They love to be a part of the community, and that includes online communities as well. The generation that has just entered the workforce and those growing up right now are very computer and internet savvy.

For the most part, this generation has been a part of those social networking sites during their schooling. These sites have provided everything from evaluations of teachers, classes, entertainment events, self advertising, keeping up with the latest school rumors, and even schools providing their school event calendars.

When this generation is out of school they become involved in all kinds of activities online, from shopping and downloading music to participating in social networks. The kids are networking socially for different reasons than adults, but both have learned to participate.

Social-Media Strategies

So you have a website and you need to market it. Using social media is different than most marketing techniques you are taught in economics or marketing in college – At least until they stop using 15-year-old text books. Now there are thousands of sites and you can make your own social media components, but the goals are the same. In the end your goals are to:

- **Know how to target your audience and deliver the right message:** If you approach the wrong audience with the wrong message, you'll learn a quick lesson in reputation management when the court of opinion attempts to destroy your reputation.
- **Create valuable content:** Good content is key to social-media marketing. If you make it a point to create fresh, unique content regularly, visitors will come to you because they know they can find the current information they need. If you're afraid of giving away all your eggs except on a one on one sales call, you will get your message out very slowly.
- **Be a valuable resource, even if it doesn't help you monetarily:** If you try to help without expecting anything in return you gain points and you can gain a good reputation which will, in turn, draw users to your website. Always wearing your salesman hat works in the corporate world, but online it is a death sentence.
- **Be a user resource:** Internet users, and especially those users who participate in social media and social networking, expect you to provide information that is useful and relevant to them. If you're not providing accurate and helpful information, they'll go to someone who is and bad mouth you on the way.
- **Help your content spread:** One way of advertising your website's services or products discreetly is to use your trophy and

long-tail keywords in your helpful tips and comments on social media sites. Search engines also index this information and when people use search engines to search on those keywords, your blog or other social networking submissions show up. Another good tip is to collect or group your helpful information into other online content such as a PDF, an audio file, or video file which you can provide links for.

- **Increase your linkability:** You want useful information that other site owners find valuable enough to put a link on their website to yours. The linkability of your site is determined by the amount of content that you have available to users who might come from social networks. Old information that rarely changes will not help, so make sure your content is updated regularly.

- **Make bookmarking your site easy:** Don't make users try to figure out how to add your blog or site to their content feed. Post your URL or code for visitors to add you to their important links or their website. Use a tool called RSS Button Maker at www.toprankblog.com/tools/rss-buttons to create a button.

- **Reward helpful users:** If you have users that are helpful and/or send business your way, find a way to reward those users so they will continue to be helpful, especially if you made the sale.

- **Don't be afraid to try new things**: Use your creativity to do something different as often as possible. In social-media optimization, creativity is rewarded.

Social media marketing is a great tool if used wisely. It can also be a terrible one if you use it wrong. Using the wrong tactics or using them only half way will render your efforts worthless. You can also expect that it will be very hard to rebuild the trust that you destroy on the web.

There are some rules of etiquette to follow that will help you keep out of trouble. Let us take a look at those in the next section.

Social Media Etiquette

As an SEO expert, I find that companies come to me frequently because their web reputation has been injured, many times unintentionally by their own staff and sometimes through no fault of their own.

Let's take a look at a few rules of etiquette that you should follow to keep yourself from becoming a statistic in the bad category:

1. Spend some time listening to your audience before you join the conversation so you can gain an understanding of the language, the tone, and the expectations of the conversation participants.

2. After you begin to interact with social media elements, use the information that you gather watching and listening on a social networks to ensure that your strategy is targeting the correct people and that the responses to your input are positive.

3. Track your site metrics to see if there are any sudden spikes or dips in your web traffic which could indicate that your involvement is effective or ineffective.

4. Provide only content that adds value to the conversation. If your content doesn't add anything or is inaccurate, the other participants will either ignore you or begin to destroy you.

5. Use RSS feeds. RSS feeds instantly update those who have chosen to watch your content. This means that your links will spread faster than you could ever imagine.

6. Keep in mind that social media is all about relationships. Both engage in and be willing to encourage participation.

7. Make an individual approach as an expert in your service or product. Approaching as the business or company will automatically create suspicion. They may think you are just there to sell something. If you don't have the time yourself, consider hiring bloggers or others to handle your company's social-media participation.

Social Media Outlets

There are many types of social media elements out there in the web world for you to tap into. It is sometimes referred to as Web 2.0 and is definitely the major shift in SEO right now. Web 2.0 is all about the social nature of the internet, and if you don't tap into that social aspect, the SEO on your site will quickly be out-of-date and ranked very low on every major search engine. Using social-media elements, however, you can get a jump-start on your social-media strategy.

So where do you start? Here are some suggestions on what sites you should visit and incorporate into your website:

- ✓ **Angies List:** www.angieslist.com
- ✓ **Blogger:** www.blogger.com
- ✓ **Blogspot:** www.blogspot.com
- ✓ **CitySearch:** www.citysearch.com
- ✓ **Customer Lobby:** www.customerlobby.com
- ✓ **Delicious Bookmarks**: www.delicious.com
- ✓ **Digg:** www.digg.com
- ✓ **Google Plus:** https://plus.google.com
- ✓ **HOUZZ:** www.houzz.com (For builders & remodelers)

- ✓ **Twitter:** www.twitter.com
- ✓ **Pintrest:** www.pintrest.com
- ✓ **Facebook:** www.facebook.com
- ✓ **LinkedIn:** www.linkedin.com
- ✓ **Merchant Circle:** www.merchantcircle.com
- ✓ **StumbleUpon:** www.stumbleupon.com
- ✓ **Reddit:** www.reddit.com
- ✓ **Yelp:** www.yelp.com
- ✓ **YouTube:** www.youtube.com
- ✓ **Wikipedia:** www.wikipedia.com

These sites each have a different social media element which can be incorporated into your website. But here is a little tip! In SEO circles the saying goes, "The more you do with Google, the more Google will do for you." It couldn't be more true in social media either. Why am I telling you this? Well from that list above, Google owns and runs Google+, Blogger.com, Blogspot.com and YouTube.com. It also heavily barrows information from Yelp. So if you're just starting with social media elements, which do you think will give you the greatest rankings on Google? You're right, brain scientist, the ones owned by Google.

Chapter 8-SEO Goals

For most people the goal is simple, outdo what your competition does for the same keywords and beat their rankings. So I guess the chapter is done. Well, maybe it's not that simple. Maybe I should break it down just a little.

Before we begin, you should have a search engine optimization plan in place. This will help you create your SEO goals. This will help your focus as the purpose of making critical changes to your website for optimization.

Your SEO plan should be updated every 3 months based on what your competition is doing versus what your previous changes have accomplished. In the next chapter, we will look at website analytics which will help you understand where your needs are. It will also help you see where you need to concentrate your efforts at any given time.

Before reading this chapter, however, you should have a good understanding of your trophy keywords and the other keywords you want to focus on. If you don't, you should visit Chapter 2 and make sure you know the keywords your company needs to use and the competition that is competing for those keywords.

In the beginning, you are most likely going to be focusing your SEO on getting your site listed on all the search engines. For this part, Chapter 3 should be your first stop. If you haven't done all the steps outlined in Chapter 3, then you should stop now and jump back there and make sure that your website's URL is listed on all the hand submissions and you have your website being submitted through automation to all the other smaller search engines and directories.

By now you should be familiar with the focus of the other chapters. We have already talked about adding your keywords into the content of each page and making each page focused on one subject, getting relevant links to your website, adding keywords to the content of each page, adding Meta tags, adding correct titles with keywords, adding multimedia, adding social media, and providing the correct word density on each page for a focused search engine.

Each one of these components is a must on your website and is all a part of your SEO strategy. These are all a part of your SEO plan and all of these components are an "add it once and forget about it" type of deal. You need to continuously monitor what is working, what is not, what your competition is doing, and make adjustments as necessary to maintain and update the elements of SEO that help you rank well.

The basic rule here is that your efforts will change, but they will never end. You need to plan to continue using, modifying, and updating your website to help your SEO rankings, and changing your strategies based on search engine changes, new internet components, etc.

For instance, last year having Twitter and RSS feeds on your website did virtually nothing for rankings. The year before having a YouTube video on your website did almost nothing for rankings. This year they are an absolute must-have to increase rankings.

This year a major change took place. Bing didn't even exist last year and our recommendation was to focus your SEO strategies only on Google with Yahoo! as an afterthought. Now because of all the changes, you might actually get more business by optimizing for Bing than your ever realized. Bing has a major market share now. With a majority of the website optimized for Google and not Bing, there is market share to gain by optimizing for Bing, especially in the very competitive keyword arena where the competition is higher than most for a keyword.

Today, every major search engine focuses on many components of a website in ranking a website. Only a few of the smaller search engines focus on a single aspect of a website their rankings. This means that over time, if you are focused only on a single keyword or links for your website, you will find that your SEO efforts will begin to fail quickly.

You have to keep your efforts up and not let down your guard. You can spend a year getting your website's rankings high and be on the first page for any search with your keywords only to lose everything in a week. The fact is you can spend months getting your rankings up and they can be lost in a fleeting moment if you are not careful.

Let me give you an example. There is a very large software company that I do the SEO for. I spent a year and a half getting them to a Google ranking of 8 out of 10. It was one of my most prized accomplishments and I jumped for joy and bragged to everyone I worked with the day I looked and their website ranking was an 8/10 on Google. Only a month later they were a PageRank of 2. So what happened?

Someone took over their website development who didn't have a clue about SEO. The new designer worked with the owner of the company to create a flashy new website without any consultation from me. In fact, my point of contact with the company didn't even know it was being done. The new website was all Flash and looked great.

The trouble is that when it was created, none of my SEO work was incorporated into the website. Even worse, the new web designer changed all the page file names for every page that was indexed with the search engines. So when users on the search engines searched on their keywords and clicked on a link to their website, there was no page. Rather, there was an error saying the page didn't exist. They were now invisible on the internet. Sales dropped to all time lows in a single month. It was two weeks before someone at my office noticed what was going on and contacted the company. By then it was too late.

When you went to their "About Us" page that used to be named "aboutus.html" it went to an error page because the new web developer named the file "about_us.php". This happened four months ago and they have reverted back to the old site as the SEO work I needed wouldn't incorporate into the new site. Search engines don't like websites that change their URL of their pages and ranking really is based on URL and not actually by website. Each page on your website has its own ranking from Google based on its relevance and all the other items we discuss in this book.

Today, the software company website that was once on the first page of every major search engine for their keywords is on page 3 of Google and has a ranking of 4/10. Their sales went from averaging 150-200 sales per month to only 63 last month. This was a catastrophe for them. They were on an uphill trend adding new employees and growing all because of the SEO work I was doing for them. Today they are four employees fewer and just barely staying in business.

A website needs constant growth and relevant material constantly to maintain its SEO status and keep the site from becoming what is known to search engines as a stale website. (A website where the material never changes.) Those changes, however, need to be looked at from an SEO optimization perspective from every angle. Most outsiders think that every web designer is familiar with SEO. From my experience, very few have any knowledge of it. It is a specialization that most web designers and developers know little or nothing about.

So what should your SEO Plan include? Let's look at this in the next section.

Time and Effort in an SEO Plan

The first thing your plan needs to include is lots of time. Then add more time to that. This is one of the main reasons that most companies sub out their SEO work. Not only because it takes someone who lives and breathes SEO to keep up on the latest trends and technology, but because of the amount of time involved.

Simply adding new content here and there on your website and changing a Meta tag or two won't help you increase your rankings on the major search engines.

> **NOTE:** *If you are doing the SEO yourself, to keep pace and save some time, you might consider designing your site similar to a blog where content is easily changeable.*

Your SEO plan should be considered a dynamic document that changes all the time based on your needs assessed from monitoring not only your website, but the search engines and your competition on the search engines. If you can't figure out what your competition is doing to one up your SEO work, then you need to call in a professional and you need to do it fast because what you do today has virtually no effect on search engines for months. In essence, you are planning today what you want to happen on the search engines 3-6 months from now. An SEO plan will help you stay on track.

Now that you understand how important it is to put time into your website's SEO, we need to create a clearly defined goal built around your business needs. Virtually every business has different needs and at different levels even when two different company websites are in the same industry.

A small local business would focus only on the local area long-tail keyword searches, whereas a large business selling nationally or in a large geographical area would need to invest time, money, and considerable effort into increasing the exposure of their website to potential customers outside its geographic region on a larger level using more generic shorter keywords.

For example, if you sell sports equipment in Portland Oregon, you would target a local campaign using the keyword of "Portland sports equipment." If your website sold sports equipment nationally you would target a much harder SEO keyword with more competition such as, "sports equipment". The fewer the words, the harder it is to get your site listed higher in the search engines. The broader the keyword, the more competition there is for that keyword.

In Portland, Oregon there are probably 40 websites competing for sports equipment and maybe ten percent do any professional website optimization. However, nationwide there are probably thousands vying for first place with those keywords and if only ten percent do website optimization, you have a lot of competition to beat.

Both the smaller company and the larger company need to implement an SEO plan. The larger company that needs to concentrate on a national level with lots of competition will require more than this book can offer (unless you are just starting your website).

If you are trying to do a national campaign with lots of competition, most likely your competition is employing powerhouse professional help. This is not the time to experiment. Your revenue (the money you make from your website) is an important factor. Your SEO plan and goals should not only focus on increasing your website visits, but also on increasing your revenues. You can track revenue by funneling your website visitors through individually targeted sales transaction pages while they are visiting your website.

You should make sure the goals you set are realistic. It's very easy to become unfocused with your SEO efforts and get discouraged when those efforts don't meet your goals or expectations. It's very easy to spend gobs of money on SEO and never accomplish anything.

Your SEO goals and the plan you create must be flexible and grow with your organization.

SEO Plan Details

Now that you have a set of goals in mind for your website, it's time to create an SEO plan. The SEO plan is the document that you'll use to help you stay focused as you try to implement your individual SEO strategies.

Keyword Research

Continuous keyword research should be your second line item after your time entry on your SEO plans details. Google Analytics (discussed in the next chapter) has a way of looking to see what keywords were used to find your site. Many times it becomes clear that there are a market of people who find your site that you didn't even know.

I will give you an example. My SEO website targets many keywords, but I noticed that several people searching for better website rankings searched using the keyword "search engine help" and found my website way down on the list of a search engine. After a few of these in one month, I added the keyword to my PPC campaign. After getting about 80 hits from that in one month, I optimized a landing page just for that keyword. I now get about 200 hits per month from that term which is business I never would have gotten had I not been analyzing the keywords people were using to access my site.

It was a minor change in the bigger picture. I was already creating content for the site, but by focusing on some of the most logical and well known keywords. I didn't crawl in the mind of a prospective searcher but Google caught it for me. I just had to interpret the results.

You should never discount the little things. Even minor details, such as refocusing and changing your keyword efforts or modifying the tagging on your pages can have a major impact if it is done right. For every website that I do SEO, I find a little niche on a monthly basis that my clients' competition never catches and I capitalize on that. Using those little niches in the right places can make a major difference in the amount of traffic that your site receives.

Reputation Management

The next item you should have in your plan is reputation management, which is a critical part of any online business. If you Google anyone of my SEO client's URL's, you see nothing but good or neutral press. The top 10 results of a search are usually corporate sites, blogs, press releases and other landing pages I optimized or created for them. This is no accident. Many clients who do any volume of online sales will get a disgruntled customer or two and sometimes a negative news article or blog entry or other problem can affect their online reputation.

Sometimes this bad press is known when it comes out in a news article that everyone sees and talks about. Sometimes, however, a disgruntled person can place negative information on blogs, as comments, and many other places that can be indexed into the search engines and work to destroy your online presence little by little. If you do not take time to monitor you SERP (Search Engine Results Page), you may miss the reason you are dropping in sales or hits to your website because of the negative that is displayed. In one case I had a customer who owned a large mortgage company. Their company does about 8,000 loans per year and have to turn down some clients for a loan, often at the last minute because of some unforeseen issue such as the client used a credit card or bought a car and dropped their credit scores, disqualifying them for the loan product for which they had been approved. It was inevitable, like it or not, that those few disturbed clients who posted their comments on blogs managed to fill up four of the top ten spots on a Google search for many of their important keywords.

Then the inevitable happened. The web visits stopped and the phone calls stopped coming. This is a good example of what can happen if you don't have monitoring your online reputation a part of your SEO plan. You're probably saying, this is nice to tell me but where do I start if I find negative links or information about my company?

Before this ever happens, you should identify key editorial contacts at industry and business publications, ezines, and press release portals that can help to place positive press in its place. Make a separate page in your plan to log these contacts. You should always be looking for opportunities to post comments on relevant articles and place links to your company's URL.

Today, you can publish stories in minutes, versus days, weeks or months. So when you do post content, it not only appears on the Website, but on search engines, syndicated content sites, and news search engines as well.

You should always create targeted press releases that can be linked-to from a variety of sources. The press release should also be optimized for the best relevant keyword density so it appears as high as possible in related searches. If you skipped learning about keyword density, there is an index in the back of this book. I would recommend learning about how to use that to your advantage.

Launch your own blog and become friendly with other bloggers, because bloggers are the most publicized arm of social online media. Bloggers are increasing their credibility with the consumer, which means their opinions really do matter. This is somewhat like a "Third Party Endorsement." Having bloggers post negative comments about you or your brand can spell disaster. Be prepared to get into the conversation by posting comments on blogs with negative content about your product/services and link back to your own press release or blog.

Another very effective tool is the use of sub-domains. Google sees them as separate websites, but they do still carry the authority and trust of the root domain. When you create a sub-domain, you must not simply copy content from your main domain. The content must be different. The new sub-domain must have useful, unique content. It does not need 100 pages; just ten or so pages per sub-domain will do. All you need is two to three well-optimized sub-domains.

Sign up for a Twitter account and place the Twitter Wiki on your website, but keep updating it with relevant information about your site. You might also consider MySpace and Facebook, or other social bookmarking network entries. And of course, post links to your press releases using keywords in your text links.

Managing your reputation requires the creation of relative content on your own website, distribution of positive content, as well as strategic participation in online discussions. When you combine these strategies, an integrated search engine reputation management program is in place and ready for action in the event a negative piece of information is indexed about your company or URL.

PPC

Monitoring your PPC account is, of course, important. Whether you use Google AdWords or Bing's AdCenter or related pay-per-click programs to get your message out there you need to constantly monitor which keywords are working for you and which ones get a lot of clicks but don't turn into sales. Too broad of a keyword, as we learned in previous chapters, can cost you a lot of money with very little results.

In terms of reputation management, a PPC campaign can help as well. While optimized press releases and related content may take days or weeks to appear high in relevant search results on search engines, paid text ads are virtually instantaneous and provide total control over placement (by keyword) of your message.

Reprioritizing Pages

In the beginning, prioritizing your web pages is easy. Give priority to the pages that focus on each of your keywords, and in the same order that your keywords are in. You should prioritize your efforts on the pages that support those trophy words and draw the most amount of traffic and sales.

These are top-priority pages and visitors should naturally gravitate to those pages. These should be focused landing pages that utilize all the optimization techniques, including social media and keyword density optimization. The content should remain relevant and constantly be updated so it never gets stale.

Pages such as your home landing page or those that will generate the most traffic or revenue should be a road map and included in your SEO plan and goals should be set for your marketing efforts. If four of the web pages on your site are your top priority, those should encompass a majority of your time and efforts in your SEO plan.

Additional Plan Items

After you have prioritized your sites web pages, you should assess where you stand and where you need to be with your current SEO efforts. Make a checklist and dedicate time to assess all the pages in your website. Those that should be checked more frequently are the following:

- Keywords(Focus 1 keyword on each optimized page.)
- Keyword density
- Local Submissions
- Online Reviews
- Title tags
- Social media elements
- Site/page tagging
- Page content relevancy
- Replacement of stale content
- Frequently changed content
- Blogs
- Social media optimization
- Social bookmarking
- Site linking
- Press release writing
- Article submissions
- Video optimization
- RSS Feeds
- Search engine placement
- PPC

Items that can be checked less frequently:

- Site map accuracy
- Longevity of domain registration
- Robots.txt optimization
- Site map
- HTML source code and errors
- Alt tags
- Link development
- Manual link requests to related sites
- Directory listings
- One-way links/two-way links
- HTML design
- ASP. and other coding such as Java and Flash
- Linked URLs

Completing the Plan

At this point you should have collected all the information you need to put into your SEO plan. You should also have a good idea of the priority of each item and what needs to be done frequently and which ones can be done on a less frequent basis to increase or maintain your website's search engine rankings.

Now it's time to put all of the information that you've gathered into a comprehensive plan comparing your available time and determining the SEO efforts you should be making to best utilize that time. Your SEO plan is more than just a simple picture of what's included in your website and what's not. This is the document you should use to help determine your website's current search engine rankings, reputation management, your needed marketing efforts, capital expenditures, time frames, and how you're going to keep your website from becoming stale.

The plan should look much like a business plan when you are done. It includes your goals, a work plan, marketing information, how you will grow your business, plans for managing problems, and much more.

Those strategies can include efforts such as manually submitting your site or pages from your site to directories and planning the content you'll use to draw search engine bots, spiders, and crawlers. It should also outline which pay-per-click programs you plan to use and a time line for the testing and implementation of those efforts, as well as regular follow-ups.

I always recommend that you supplement your SEO with a well-managed PPC campaign. But the goal is to maintain your URL on the first page of a search engine's search using organic SEO to maximize those naturally occurring elements. When you build on each internal and external element on your website to create a site that will naturally fall near the top of the search engine results pages (SERPs), you achieve high SERPs rankings free — other than the time it takes to implement your SEO plan.

Achieving each ranking point for organic SEO can take anywhere from three to eight months if you implement the right SEO plan. Don't get upset if you don't see immediate results from your SEO efforts. Stick to your SEO plan. If you don't see changes within 3-6 months or your rankings get worse, you should reevaluate your SEO plan or seek professional help.

Chapter 9 – Black Hat Tactics Will Get You In Trouble

I have so many instances and references where I myself have made mistakes or where others have fallen before me and I have learned from their mistakes. In this chapter we will talk about many of what are known as black hat tactics which you should avoid:

- Flash
- AJAX
- Complex Java Script Menus
- Dynamic URL's
- Dynamic Code On Pages
- Bad XML Site Maps
- Abnormal Keyword Placement
- SEO Spam
- Doorway Pages
- Meta Jacking
- Page Cloaking
- IP Delivery/Page Cloaking
- Link Farms
- Spamblogs
- Page Highjacking
- Sybil Attacks
- Link Bombing
- What to Do If You Have Been Banned
- Problem Pages and Work-Arounds
- Validating Your HTML

Flash

When used correctly, it can enhance a visitor's experience, unless you're trying to get mobile devices to be compatible. The non-mobile side of your website shouldn't be built entirely in Flash, nor should your site navigation be done only in Flash. Search engines have claimed for a couple years now that they're better at crawling Flash, but it's still not a substitute for good, crawlable site menus and content.

AJAX

The same issues mentioned regarding Flash apply here to AJAX. Google has now claimed it can read AJAX and index what it has found but I have not been able to find any examples of this. AJAX can add to your site's user experience, but AJAX has historically not been visible to search engine crawlers. In order to let Google to index your AJAX website content, Google offers guidelines to help make AJAX-based content crawlable, but it's complicated and the SEO "best practice" recommendations remain the same. Don't put important or unique content in AJAX.

Complex Java Script menus

Javascript is another technology that search engines are getting better at crawling, but is still best avoided as the primary method of presenting site navigation. Google has explained:

While we are working to better understand JavaScript, your best bet for creating a site that's crawlable by Google and other search engines is to provide HTML links to your content.

That's still the best practice today: Make sure your site navigation is presented in simple, easy-to-crawl HTML links.

Dynamic URL's

A "dynamic URL" is most simply defined as one that has a "?" in it, like

http://www.yourdomain.com/page.src?ID=3456

That's a very simple dynamic URL and today's search engines have no trouble crawling something like that. But when dynamic URLs get longer and more complicated, search engines may be less likely to crawl them (for a variety of reasons, one of which is that studies show searchers prefer short URLs). So, if your URLs look anything like this, you may have crawlability problems:

http://www.yourdomain.com/page.src?ID=3456&XID=9765487&CID=3333 94445&VID=34521456&SESSION=875694875

Google's webmaster help page says it well: "…be aware that not every search engine spider crawls dynamic pages as well as static pages. It helps to keep the parameters short and the number of them few."

Dynamic Code On Pages

Code that is held in a database and pages that display the output dynamically and on pages that deliver unique output will have issues being indexed by the search engines. Some pages also have what is termed as "code bloat."

Code bloat is situations where the code required to render your page is dramatically more substantial than the actual content of the page. In many cases, this is not something you'll need to worry about—search engines have gotten better at dealing with pages that have heavy code and little content.

Robots.txt Blocking

First, you are not required to have a robots.txt file on your website; millions of websites are doing just fine without one. But if you use one (perhaps because you want to make sure your Admin or Members-only pages aren't crawled), be careful not to completely block spiders from your entire website. It's easy to do with just a simple line of code.

In no circumstances should your robots.txt file have something like this:

User-agent: *
Disallow: /

That code will block all bots, crawlers, and spiders from accessing your website. If you ever have questions about using a robots.txt file, visit robotstxt.org.

Bad XML Site Map

An XML sitemap lets you give a list of URLs to search engines for possible crawling and indexing. They're not a replacement for correct on-site navigation and not a cure-all for situations where your website is difficult to crawl.

If implemented properly, an XML sitemap can help search engines become aware of content on your site that they may have missed. But, if implemented incorrectly, the XML sitemap might actually deter bots, crawlers, and spiders from crawling.

If you're curious, I've only once recommended that a client use XML sitemaps, and that was a website with upwards of 15 million pages. If you need to get a professionally created XML sitemap, you can have one created at **www.smcreator.com**.

Abnormal Keyword Delivery

The reason I am discussing this first is because it is the most common occurrence. I read all the time on SEO blogs that a person got his website on the first page of Google by placing his keywords a hundred times at the bottom of his website landing page in text that was the same color as the background of his website. The person is so excited that he discounts and ignores all the professionals who comment that he shouldn't do this. Sometime the blog creator or commenter who has his site on the first page of Google even bad mouths the SEO professionals trying to help him.

I come back and read all the time how just a few short months later, the same guy that was so excited that his website was on the first page of Google has written, "You guys were right. Google banned my URL for doing this." It is easy to temporarily be the most relevant site on Google the wrong way. But Google and the other major search engines have ways of figuring it out quite quickly. And once you are banned, you better call in the pros to help you. There is a section dedicated to this as the end of this chapter.

SEO Spam

SEO spam is the SEO version of email spam. Email spam pops up in your inbox where it's least wanted and those who are sending it believe that the law of averages is on their side. They think if you send out enough messages, eventually someone will respond.

SEO spam uses the same principle, except SEO spam fills the search engine results pages on search engines with results that have little or no value to the searcher. This can get you quickly banned. Imagine if you went to Google and every time you did a search you got results that were for something totally different than you searched for, or if the top 10 spaces of the search results were filled with the same company. If that happened you would switch to Bing in a heartbeat to get better results. Right?

Google and the other major search engines don't want this to happen. So if you do something that a search engine sees as spamming, your search rankings will be penalized. It's now even more likely that you will be removed from search rankings entirely. If Google bans your URL it's as if you website has been removed from the internet. It is almost invisible.

A term for some SEO spam is called *black hat SEO*. Black hat SEO refers to the use of aggressive SEO strategies, techniques and tactics that focus only on search engines and not a human audience. Some examples of black hat SEO techniques include keyword stuffing, link farms, invisible website text and doorway pages, which we will learn about later in this chapter.

Black Hat SEO is more frequently used by those who are looking for a quick financial return rather than a long-term investment on their website.

> **NOTE:** *Black Hat SEO will most likely result in your URL being banned from major search engines. However, since the focus is usually on quick high return business models, most experts who use Black Hat SEO tactics consider being banned from search engines a somewhat irrelevant risk. Black Hat SEO may also be referred to as Unethical SEO or just spamdexing.*

To make things a little more perplexing, search engines change their definitions of spam regularly. What works and is acceptable today may well be classified as spam tomorrow. This can have a profound effect on your rankings. One day you may be ranked high and on page one of a search and the next you may find that you're on page 8 of the results all because of the links you maintain.

The easiest way to monitor search engine changes is to keep up with what's happening in SEO on the Google Webmaster Central Blog (http://googlewebmastercentral.blogspot.com/). You can also learn about what's changing on ISEdb–Internet Search Engine Database (www.isedb.com), High Rankings Advisor (www.highrankings.com), and SEONews.com.

The general rule is, if you're doing something on your website that you have to worry might get you banned from major search engines, you probably shouldn't be doing it.

If you read anywhere that SEO spam techniques are okay, or that you won't get caught because search engines don't pay attention, ignore this advice at all costs. The penalties differ according to the search engine, but if you are caught spamming even once, most search engines will delist you from search results immediately. I have seen it a hundred times and have had it happen to me on accident when I went overboard experimenting. Yes, even the experts make a mistake or two. But we learn from them.

Here's what is definitely considered spam:

- Trying to make your site appear more relevant to the search engines by embedding hidden keywords in your website.
- Artificially generating links to your website from unrelated sites for the purpose of increasing your ranking based on link analysis.

- Artificially generating traffic to your website so that it appears more popular than it really is.
- Submitting your website repeatedly for inclusion in the rankings.

NOTE: *You should submit your site once and then wait at least six weeks before submitting it again.*

Doorway Pages

Doorway pages are created to do well for particular phrases. They are also known as portal pages, jump pages, bridges, gateway pages, entry pages, and by other names as well. Search engines have developed ways to easily identify these pages. They are primarily to make a page seem more relevant for search engines, and not for human beings.

You should always have your pages designed for human eyes and not just for a search engine. There are various ways to deliver doorway pages. The low-tech way is to create and submit a web page that is targeted toward a particular phrase or keyword.

These pages tend to be very generic. It's easy for people to copy them, make minor changes, and submit the revised page. Sometimes these are so similar that the search consider these duplicates and automatically exclude them from their listings.

Another problem is that users sometimes arrive at the doorway page. Say a real person searched for "welding supplies" and the doorway page appears. They click through, but that page probably lacks any detail about the welding supplies that you sell. To get them to that content, webmasters usually propel visitors forward with a prominent "Click Here" link or with an automatic page redirect.

Some search engines no longer accept pages using any redirects (sometimes referred to as fast Meta refresh). This has led to some black hatters doing a bait-and-switch, or "code-swapping," on the search engines. Some black hat webmasters submit a real web page, wait for it to be indexed and then swap it with a doorway page.

The trouble is that a search engine may revisit at any time figure out what you have done.

Meta Jacking

Meta jacking is the taking of the Meta tagging from one page and placing them on another page hoping to obtain good rankings and relevance.

However, simply taking Meta tags from a page will not guarantee a page will do well. In fact, sometimes resubmitting the exact page from another location does not gain the same position as the original page.

Agent Delivery

When you target a single doorway page to a single search engine this is called "agent delivery." Each search engine reports an "agent" name, just as each browser reports a name.

Agent delivery pages are tailored pages that direct users to the actual content you want them to see. It also has the added benefit of "cloaking" your code from only the search engine you are targeting. The major search engines have gotten wise to this, though. They change the name they report specifically to help keep people honest.

IP Delivery / Page Cloaking

To avoid the agent name changing, you can also deliver pages to the search engines by allowing only the search engines IP address. If a bot, crawler, or spider visits your doorway page and reports an IP address that matches the search engine's or the IP resolves to a certain host name, it can see the code of the website.

Link Farms

Link farms are simply pages of links that are created just to artificially boost a linking strategy in an effort to speed the appearance of the website in the top search ranking positions. Typically you pay money to join them or buy software that allows you to mass send your links.

Spamblogs

These are software or machine-generated blogs which have only one purpose – increase search engine rankings.

Page Highjacking

Page hijacking occurs when very popular webpage coding is stolen and used to represent your website to the search engines. When users perform a search and see your webpage in the search results, they click through the link only to be taken to your actual page.

Sybil Attacks

Sybil attacks are when a spammer creates multiple websites that are all interlinked for the purpose of creating a false link structure. These are sometimes called incestuous links.

Link Bombing

One anchor text tactic to avoid is link bombing . Link bombing refers to the methods used by black hat SEOs to artificially inflate their website ranking by connecting an unrelated keyword to a specific website. For link bombing to work, more than one website designer must be willing to participate in a link exchange.

What to Do If You Have Been Banned

If you have been banned from the major search engines, you may find it the worst experience of your life, especially since the internet is now the official yellow pages for most and being banned from the major search engines is like locking your business doors and taking the phone off the hook.

Most of the time you will know what was done that got you banned. In this case, it may require explaining to the search engine the tactic you employed, why you employed it, and how you fixed it. Google, for instance, allows you to send in an explanation by going to the

Google Webmaster Tools (https://www.google.com/webmasters/tools) and clicking on the "Site Reconsideration" link on the left-hand side. This will take you to the web page which outlines written and video instructions to resubmit your website.

It could take a couple of months to a year to be reindexed into the search engine. In some cases it is quicker and easier to ditch the old URL and start a brand new one. Then you have to work your way back to the top of the rankings again. Just make sure that you have fixed or stopped doing whatever was done to get your URL banned in the first place.

Outgoing Link Issues

Linking out is crucial for blogs and even static websites. Many webmasters stopped linking out in order to hoard PageRank and not allow others in their industry to get a better rank. Google engineers absolutely discourage this practice. In fact, so much so that Google has started to really want to see industry related links that are two-way links on not only the homepage but the deep pages as well. Linking out can be risky though. Here are some things to look out for.

Broken links

Too many broken links on a page raise a red flag in the Google algorithm, so you need to make sure your links going out, are always good. This might not be a penalty in the strictest sense, but you drop suddenly in rankings once more than one or two links are broken on the same page.

Links To Bad Neighborhoods

Bad neighborhoods are server IP addresses that host websites Google finds bad. Such as porn sites, hate sites, some political sites, spammers etc. Most of these links happen more naturally as part of link decay. Sites disappear and domain grabbers buy them to display ad loaded "domain parking" pages. These pages can be bad as well.

Too Many Outbound Links Can Be Bad, As Well As None At All

This figure changes, but currently our testing shows, Google is fine with up to 76 outbound links on a page but degrades the pages ranking after this number. A website that has more outgoing links than content itself can lose its search visibility. This might not happen overnight like the typical penalty you'd expect, but it can amount to one in its effects. Also, pages without a single outbound link are now being termed "dead-ends". In this case there are no outbound links and Google has been placing a severe penalty on these pages.

Hidden Links

This may sound crazy. How do you hide a link? Well in add-ons, in CSS coding, etc. I am adding this section because of a counter added to a WordPress website that contained a links in it to other websites. The link was not only hidden; but was absolutely spammy. We couldn't figure ot the source of the problem until an AccuQuality.com report we ran on the website revealed the over 180 outbound links and the reason Google was penalizing the website.

Content

Google consistently stresses that "content is king", but it also can mean trouble. If there is no king in your kingdom, or the king is dressed in rags, or you borrowed you king from somewhere else you look bad to Google. Here are some content issues you should look out for:

> **Duplicate content** – duplicate content on your own site or even elsewhere can result in a significant ranking drop. While Google does not consider this a penalty, most webmasters who experience the problem do.

> **Low quality content** – Google's high quality update dubbed Panda and it later updates, focuses on low quality content. Shallow, keyword-rich content on some pages can make your whole site drop in Google.

> **Scraped content** – Scraped content is text taken from other sites and displayed on yours, is a surefire way to get deranked very quickly.

> **Unlegible content** – Content that is written in broken English or misspelled can hurt you badly.   So much so that AccuQuality.com now spells checks your entire website in their report.   As a general rule, your content needs sound good to the human visitor as much as to the search engines crawler who is visiting.

Ads

Google is not really a search engine but an advertising company as almost all revenue of the Google corporation stem from ads displayed in the search results themselves and on third party sites. Nonetheless, the pressure on Google has grown over the years to tackle the problem of so called MFA (Made for Adsense) sites that pollute the Google index. With Google "Panda" the search giant finally did tackle this issue. So this means there are some new rules to follow:

> **Too many ads (low content to ads ratio)** – ever since Google "Panda" has been the talk of the town, most pundits have pointed out that a too high number of ads, especially Google AdSense ads, may lead to a penalty.

Affiliate sites with no value – Google always explained that affiliates are not an issue, but only as long as they offer some good content and additional value beyond the actual affiliate offer. Be sure to add different content, products, or services or you will face a penalty sooner or later.

Bad Press Or A Bad Online Reputation

The issue of so-called "SEO outing" has been a hot one in 2011, as numerous high profile websites have been ousted and along with them their SEO teams or companies. Many SEO practitioners argue on moral grounds that outing is a despicable practice. They might be right, but as long as there is nothing to out you, fare best. So you'd better manage your reputation online and from time to time check what the SEO team does.

NYT and WSJ

High profile old media outlets like the NYT (New York Times) and the WSJ (Wall Street Journal) like to scandalize SEO, so if you get a call from a journalist you'd better not brag about your great SEO tactics. Google, in most cases, reacts to high profile outings aka bad press.

Third party trust metrics like Blekko, WOT, McAfee Siteadvisor

If you don't show up in Blekko, because you are banned there, and when sites like WOT and SiteAdvisor lists your site as deceptive or dangerous, this might mean you are heading towards a Google penalty. Google does not use these sites' data but has other means to screen the Web for the same issues.

Making Google look stupid

You do not need an NYT article, a SEO blogger or Google employee to get penalized for a bad rep. Publicly showing off your black hat SEO successes makes you vulnerable to the "making Google look stupid" penalty. Leading SEO specialists agree that from a certain point on, Google can't keep quiet about it and will penalize you in order to keep its face.

Technical issues

Not every sudden drop in rankings and traffic is a penalty; some are stupidity or gross negligence. You can shoot yourself in the foot by messing with some technical aspects of web development.

Robots.txt

The robots.txt is not really needed to improve SEO. It can break a lot of things though. Just recently I blocked one of my blogs from being indexed by Google. Of course I suspected a penalty at first but then checked Google Webmaster Tools to find out I made the mistake.

No follow

I've seen leading blogs barred from the Google index because they activated the WordPress privacy mode. It simply meant that all of the blog was set to noindex, nofollow which equals blocking it in the robots.txt.

Duplicate titles and descriptions

When your site uses the same or a very similar page title and description for every single page, it's no wonder most of them won't show up in search results. This isn't a penalty either. It's just logical.

Non-crawlable links in JavaScript

There are still JavaScript site menus out there that can't get crawled by Google. Always check whether your menu uses real HTML links with "<a href="">" in it. Or at least the whole URL must show up.

Neither a penalty Or Your Fault

In some cases a loss of rankings or search traffic has nothing to do with you or your site. Something else changed instead, and that's why you get outranked all of a sudden.

Algorithm changes

Google changes and refines its algorithm all the time. Major changes are called updates, and sometimes mean dramatic shifts in search results. Just search for "Google Panda". The only thing you can do then is to find out what changed and why your site does not match the new ranking factors.

Competition got better

A common "problem" is also that your competition does more SEO work than you do and one day they outrank you. A ranking change from #1 to #2 on Google can mean a traffic loss of 60 to 80%.

Current events

Sometimes breaking news may push your site down. Google News results get displayed on top, and for less competitive phrases news media start to rank in regular results as well. Most of these ranking changes will vanish after a few days.

SERP display change

Google experiments all the time with its search results' display. Most notably, local results from Google Places take away large parts of the screen real estate. You might rank at #1 in organic results and still get displayed at the bottom of the search results page.

There are numerous reasons to see a search traffic slump one day out of the blue. It doesn't have to be a penalty, but if you engage in some of the high risk SEO tactics mentioned above it can be one. Make sure you have at least two web analytics tools to check what happened. Google Analytics is not perfect and sometimes the ways it measures traffic get changed overnight without notification.

Chapter 10 – Website Marketing Principles

Throughout my career I have been thought of by many as being one of the best sales persons both online and in real life. There are many things that help me make sales. In this chapter, I will outline the little things that add up one by one to help you make sales. Although the focus here is on online sales, these are sales principles that you should use every day both online and in real life to help you sell.

Sales Principles You Should Adopt

These are my top 12 direct marketing principles you can use to make sure your internet marketing really works for you:

Stability

People want to know you are not going to disappear overnight so if you have been in business for any length of time, this will add credibility to you and your offers.

Statistics

Use genuine statistics to give you more credibility when listing the number of customers served, money saved, profits made, true results, and so on.

Testimonials

I can't overestimate the importance of getting relevant and credible reviews from your customers and clients, saying how you and your products or services have helped them.

Self Credibility

If you can, establish yourself as an expert in your field. Not everyone can write numerous books or be on TV. However, you can write articles and have them published on your product, service, or industry. You can run workshops that are designed to demonstrate or train how to use your products or how effective your services are.

Reprints of articles about you in the press or having your articles published in the media lend weight to your credibility as the expert or authority in your market and are highly valuable to you. Show your market that you are in demand, and have status as an expert.

You can also show you're an expert with industry certifications, awards, memberships, and accomplishments that are relevant to your market.

Demonstrations

It is a lot cheaper to sell online with the use of online videos or 'how to' DVDs to sell your product. If you hire a sales person he can only be one place at a time. The internet can be the equivalent of hundreds of sales people. A website that is properly designed can make it very easy to show a demonstration of your product or services, both on and offline.

You can also create and distribute a demonstration eBook by printing it out and talking through what it contains live on screen. Camtasia is free software that lets you make a screen capture video where you can demonstrate your website talking though the sales letter or giving a demo of how easy it is to download your eBook.

> **NOTE:** *You can also print eBooks cost effectively at Lulu.com and CreateSpace.com.*

Guarantee

If you can't guarantee the product or service you're selling, then find something else to sell that you can guarantee. To really make your potential customers feel safe buying from you, have an ironclad guarantee.

Accessibility

On your website, having your full contact detail information is a big boost to your potential customer confidence. Using just an email contact or a form shows you are hiding. Put your email, phone, and address that shows that you are in the U.S. and are credible.

> **NOTE:** *Never give a P.O. Box as your address as it immediately makes people suspicious.*

The Personal Touch

Be visible in the business you're in and make sure you have a live voice answer your phone if possible. In my SEO business, if I let voicemail pickup for one day I never get a sale. If I answer the phone, I usually always make a sale. Also, tell your customers about yourself. Make it personal to them and show them you are a real individual.

Admit Imperfections Upfront

No matter how good your product or service is, it will most likely have a disadvantage somewhere. Admit it up front and honestly comment on this fact.

Answer questions and objections in a timely manner when a potential customer asks them via email or the phone. Buyers buy more often when they can call an office throughout the week and email at any time with questions and get a human response.

People Will Buy to Save Money

People who are interested in your product or service will usually do nothing unless you ask for the sale and give them incentive. People are just bombarded by too many sales pitches and try to choose the best one.

 The best pitch is to create urgency to buy now, such as informing them that the price is going up next week. But you have plenty of options here: you can offer a reduced price, a bundled special deal on your products or services, or a smaller free item for buying an larger item now.

Special Tactic for Creating Urgency

A special tactic to create urgency is to put an end date on your promotions and discounts – buy it now before the price goes up next week, next month, tomorrow. Even if your regular price is your promotional price, do a monthly campaign. When they look online they see a higher price if you don't buy by the end of the month.

If your business looks like it is always in permanent sale mode, there's no urgency for the customer to buy. Customers are not stupid; they see the advertising and know that this company ALWAYS has a sale on.

That is why it's important you create a deadline for your promotion. By having a defined end date showing in bold letters, it creates urgency and a reason for your potential customer to act now or lose out on saving money.

Tell People the Value They Are Getting

The discounts and value to the customer are not always obvious. So make it clear. If you put a value next to the items you are selling, don't assume your prospect or customer has worked it out for themselves. If the total value is $250, tell them it is $250 because if you leave them to add it up for themselves they generally won't do it.

Research

Research is an essential aspect of marketing. Inadequate research of your products and target market is one of the biggest pitfalls that can affect a marketing strategy. Research provides a wealth of information that is vital to your sales.

Determine what market is going to most likely benefit from the product or service you provide. This is the group of individuals you will want to target – in some areas, there may be multiple groups. While it may be possible to market to all these groups, in most situations it is better to market to a single group which contain a large percentage of similar traits. This makes it easier to consolidate a marketing plan as well as eliminate a significant amount of research, time, and effort.

The second aspect which needs to be researched for a marketing plan to be successful is your competition. It is also one of the reasons why marketing fails to produce appropriate results. Researching your competition is not just about researching the prices of a competitor. It includes noting things such as their sales techniques, finding out what marketing tools and resources they use, and how often those tools.

Many business owners and beginning internet marketers fail to note anything more than price and perhaps general layout of their competitors website and end their research there. They miss vital information that can save time, money, and effort when it comes to setting up their own marketing strategy. If you are not the most successfully-marketed business on the internet promoting your product or service, find out who is. Find out how they market and what makes them successful.

Collect information on the types of deals, offers, discounts and promotions that your competition uses and offer something different to help your business stand out. Many people simply do what their competition does. In doing so, they often lower their marketability and their marketing plan can ultimately fail in this area. You might pick up more market share by doing what the completion doesn't.

Marketing Tools

Having enough research to create your marketing plan is only the first step in solving the problems that often cause marketing plans to fail. The next step is to take the time to pick out the right tools. Having the right tools for the job is essential to ensuring you get the most out of your marketing strategies.

Marketing tools have diversified over the years. Tools are not limited strictly to email and promotional options. Video, social networking, SMS texting, Blogs, Twitter, Facebook, PPC, and many more are available to you. You just have to pick the tools that are going to be easy for you to learn, use, and require minimal maintenance with maximum potential results.

Don't Just Dream It, Do It!

One of the biggest reasons I am so successful is that if I get an idea, I do it. Nothing stands in my way. Hence you are reading this book because I came up with an idea for it while taking a shower. Don't picture that, by the way. In John Pinette's words, "You'll have nightmares!"

One of the biggest reasons why marketing strategies and businesses end up failing is lack of action and giving up. Marketing is an active part of your business, it is not a "set it in motion and let it run on its own" component of a website. In order to ensure that a marketing strategy succeeds you must be actively engaged in working that plan and revisit it and make the strategy better based on experience. This means that email marketing messages should be updated and redesigned regularly.

SMS, Facebook, and Twitter messages should be rewritten after every send. These messages should be short, contain only the minimum necessary information, and focus on one item at a time. It is important to remember that this type of marketing is relatively new and involves sending messages to Wiki's, blogs, members, and mobile devices that often indicate repeat messages.

Videos should be produced, edited, and updated to as high a level as possible. Computers and technology can turn just about any computer into a production studio with the right software. Keep videos interesting, engaging, and relevant. The videos should be related to the company, the products, or the services offered.

It is important to set up a marketing schedule and find out how much time, generally through trial and error, that you need each day, week or month to handle all your marketing tasks and keep everything up to date.

The reasons why a marketing plan might fail are numerous. I hate to outline some of them here, but you need to know so you can take steps avoid them. Some of these reasons include the following: failing to do the proper research into the market, not doing proper SEO, not having the right tools available, not researching cheaper delivery methods, having too many tools or not using the tools you have effectively, and not having inventory on hand that you are selling.

Taking the time to make sure that you have the information you need as well as putting in the effort to ensure your success can go a long way to eliminating these reasons.

When you develop a marketing message, you have to hit many levels of desire. Good marketing happens when you give logical reasons for your prospect's emotional-buying decisions. Some good marketing messages include:

- Save time
- Save money
- Make money
- Try for free
- Avoid effort
- Increase happiness
- Find success
- Be pain-free
- Get better health
- Have fun
- Enjoy your life
- Gain praise
- Feel safe and secure
- Feel liked or loved
- Be popular

Your task is to find a message which matches to your product or service and start promoting your marketing message in your marketing strategy.

See What Your Potential Clients Desire and Play on That

You should develop the ability to see what others want, need, and desire through your own research. You will be successful if you are always satisfying your customer's needs. Sometimes you have to look for the gap and create a new product or service or develop an improvement of an existing product or service.

You should always focus on service and deliver what you promise on time. My general rule is to always under promise and over deliver. Tell a customer that he/she will not have it until Friday even though it arrives on Wednesday. If something is delayed, the customer is not upset and when you deliver it early you look like the hero.

The internet allows you to start small and grow to any size business that you want to. Following the advice and principles I have laid out in this chapter will help your customer numbers grow and your profits grow with them.

Dealing With Adversity

My last words of advice are always maintain honesty and integrity in your dealings and stay true to your values even when dealing with stressful situations. Every business owner is going to have to deal with anxiety, frustration and problems, so cope with them by developing tenacity and perseverance.

If sales don't happen the first time you talk to a potential client, look at these statistics from the National Sales Executive Association:

- 2% of sales are made on the 1st contact;
- 3% of sales are made on the 2nd contact;
- 5% of sales are made on the 3rd contact;
- 10% of sales are made on the 4th contact (and)
- 80% of sales are made on the 5th – 12th contact.

For most businesses, if you don't offer an opt-in contact, like a regular email newsletter or blog postings, you're missing out on most of your potential sales.

When setting up an opt-in internet marketing campaign, you should offer incentives to subscribe. To entice people to opt-in, you can offer:

- Special pricing for email list members
- A first look at new products
- Ability for customer to select subjects and emails they receive
- Promise not to share email or other personal info with other companies

Using opt-in contact allows you to significantly increase conversions by introducing yourself over time to your potential customers, in a soft-sell manner

Website optimization is important; the goal is increased internet traffic, sales and sales leads. But whether you've hired an online SEO consultant or you're doing the process yourself, affordable search engine optimization by itself does not accomplish those last points which increase sales and sales leads. It just drives the potential customers to your website. You still have to close the deal.

Chapter 11 – Targeting More Than One Keyword

Most web sites selling anything need to target more than a single keyword. Even if you just sell a single product or service. So what do you do to promote your web site and focus on many keywords since many of the major search engines only allow a web page to be relevant for three keywords.

The answer is a simple one but the execution is about the most complex of any part of your web site's code. The answer is that you need to create a perfectly optimized landing page for every single keyword you want to focus on. You then have to have the search engines index all those additional pages separately as separate landing pages. This is the tough part. Even the singular and the plural version of your keywords need to be focused on other pages.

To be found by Google for all the different pages on your website you need to have a site map to tell the search engines the landing pages you want to index. Not just any, there is a standard called Sitemap protocol 0.90 which Google requires along with Google's many updated requirements.

> **WARNINGS:** *There are so many web sites and web developers on the Internet that claim they can create a sitemap. Many just create pages with links and call them a sitemap. Also, there has been many updates to the Sitemap Protocol and many web sites still push older versions. I highly recommend that if you are not a professional developer you go to a trusted source such as SMMaker.com or SMCreator.com and have them professionally create and install a Sitemap for your web site.*

In this chapter I am going to tell you how to make a Sitemap specially formulated to Google and Bing. And then how to tell Google and Bing where to look for your site map. As you saw from the warning above, it is a lot of work to create a site map and test it to see if it is working. It is so much easier to just visit either one of these sites and pay less than $15.00 to have it created for you at either of these web sites:

> http://www.SMMaker.com
> http://www.SMCreator.com

So let's take a look at how to create a site map.

Sitemaps XML format

Informing search engine crawlers This document describes the XML schema for the Sitemap protocol. The Sitemap protocol format consists of XML tags. All data values in a Sitemap must be entity-escaped. The file itself must be UTF-8 encoded.

The Sitemap must include the following:

- Begin with an opening <urlset> tag and end with a closing </urlset> tag.
- Specify the namespace (protocol standard) within the <urlset> tag.
- Include a <url> entry for each URL, as a parent XML tag.
- Include a <loc> child entry for each <url> parent tag.

All of the other tags are optional. Support for these optional tags may vary among search engines. Refer to each search engine's documentation for details. For Google you must include this tag:

```
<urlset xmlns="http://www.sitemaps.org/schemas/sitemap/0.9">
```

Let's look at an example which shows a Sitemap that contains just a single URL:

```
<?xml version="1.0" encoding="UTF-8"?>
<urlset xmlns="http://www.sitemaps.org/schemas/sitemap/0.9">
  <url>
    <loc>http://www.SEOForResults.com/</loc>
    <lastmod>2013-01-01</lastmod>
    <changefreq>monthly</changefreq>
    <priority>0.8</priority>
  </url>
</urlset>
```

All XML Tags

Here are all the tags that can be used in your site map and their syntaxes and descriptions.

<urlset> (required)

Encapsulates the file and references the current protocol standard.

<url> (required)

Parent tag for each URL entry. The remaining tags are children of this tag.

<loc> (required)

URL of the page. This URL must begin with the protocol (such as http) and end with a trailing slash, if your web server requires it. This value must be less than 2,048 characters.

<lastmod> (optional)

The date of last modification of the file. This date should be in W3C Date/time format. This format allows you to omit the time portion, if desired, and use YYYY-MM-DD.

<changefreq> (optional)

How frequently the page is likely to change. This value provides general information to search engines and may not correlate exactly to how often they crawl the page. Valid syntaxes are:

- always
- hourly
- daily
- weekly
- monthly
- yearly
- never

<priority> (optional)

The priority of this URL relative to other URLs on your site. Valid values range from 0.0 to 1.0. This value does not affect how your pages are compared to pages on other sites—it only lets the search engines know which pages you deem most important for the crawlers.

NOTE: *The default priority of a page is 0.5.*

The priority you assign to a page is not likely to influence the position of your URLs in a search engine's result pages. Search engines may use this information when selecting between URLs on the same site, so you can use this tag to increase the likelihood that your most important pages are present in a search index.

WARNING: *Assigning a high priority to all of the URLs on your site is not likely to help you. Since the priority is relative, it is only used to select between URLs on your site.*

Here is an example using the different tags:

```
<?xml version="1.0" encoding="UTF-8"?>
<urlset xmlns="http://www.sitemaps.org/schemas/sitemap/0.9">
<url>
<loc>http://www.seoforresults.com</loc>
<lastmod>2013-01-20</lastmod>
<priority>0.5</priority>
</url>
<url>
<loc>http://www.seoforresults.com/seo-pricelist.php</loc>
<lastmod>2013-01-20</lastmod>
<priority>0.5</priority>
</url>
<url>
<loc>http://www.seoforresults.com/SEO.php</loc>
<lastmod>2012-05-20</lastmod>
<priority>0.5</priority>
</url>
<url>
<loc>http:// www.seoforresults.com/SEM.php</loc>
<lastmod>2010-05-20</lastmod>
<priority>0.5</priority>
</url>
</urlset>
```

Saving your Site Map

Search engines know to look for a plain text site map at the root directory of your website where your Index page resides. It should be named "Sitemap.xml"

For instance it should be accessible using your site URL. If the Sitemap is located at http://www. www.seoforresults.com/sitemap.xml and it can't include URLs from http://subdomain.seoforresults.com.

You can submit a sitemap using a port. If you submit a Sitemap using a path with a port number, you must include that port number as part of the path in each URL listed in the Sitemap file. For instance, if your

Sitemap is located at:

http://www. www.seoforresults.com*:100/sitemap.xml*

Then each URL listed in the Sitemap must begin with:

http:// www.seoforresults.com*:100*

Submit Your Site Map To Google And Bing

You can submit your website's site map URL to both Google and Bing. To do this go to the following websites and login with the Google and Bing ID's you used in Chapter 3. For Google go to:

https://www.google.com/webmasters/tools/

(Go to **Site configuration**, click **Sitemaps**)

For Bing.com go to:

http://www.bing.com/webmaster

Where to go for more information

For more information on how to configure a site map visit:

http://www.sitemaps.org/schemas/sitemap/0.9/siteindex.xsd

There are a number of tools available to help you validate the structure of your Sitemap based on this schema. You can find a list of XML-related tools at the following websites:

http://www.w3.org/XML/Schema#Tools
http://www.xml.com/pub/a/2000/12/13/schematools.html

Chapter 12: The Google Toolbar And The PageRank Tool

Google provides a plug-in called the PageRank Tool on the Google Toolbar. In the past, SEO's have been rated and results have been heavily influenced by what Google calls the PageRank of a website. This then went from a websites PageRank to a tool to rank each individual page. This means that Google ranks each web page individually and the PageRank on the homepage has no real relevance to pages deeper in the website or newer pages created by the website.

Today, the positioning of a website in Google's results are hardly influenced by the PageRank given to a website or web page by Google. Google's results are really based on numerous other factors including optimization of the page, linking, relevance of the content, website coding, URL standings, and now a very important factor which we cover later social media.

Googlebot is the bot that comes to all the websites Google knows about at least once per month and looks at the coding of the website and indexes all the information as well as links the bot can find on a website. Google makes it easy to see when its Googlebot has last visited a webpage right inside the Google Toolbar.

The Google toolbar is available free of charge at:

> http://toolbar.google.com.

You download a small program, and you are ready for some easy searching. The toolbar works with Microsoft Windows NT, 2000, XP, Vista, 2003 Server, 2008 Server ,Windows 7 and 8. You must also have Microsoft Internet Explorer or Chrome installed. Google removed support for Firefox so you are out of luck with that browser. Mac users are in luck though. The Google Chrome browser is now available for the MAC but the PageRank tool is a separate plug-in and as there is no Google Toolbar for the Chrome browser.

> **TIP:** There are many Google and third party PageRank plug-in with many special features for the Windows and MAC Chrome browsers available from the Google Chrome Store at:

> https://chrome.google.com/webstore/search/pagerank

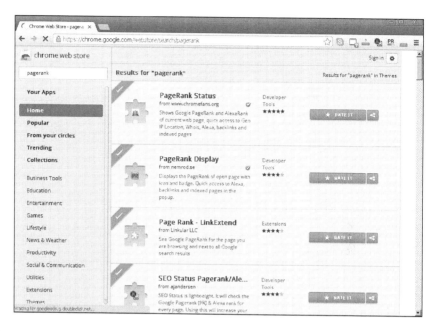

Installing The Google PageRank Tool On The Google Toolbar

Now you have to install the PageRank Tool in Google Toolbar as it is not available by default. To do this in Internet Explorer you have to click on the little wrench on the right side of the Google Toolbar.

Then select the Privacy Tab as seen below.

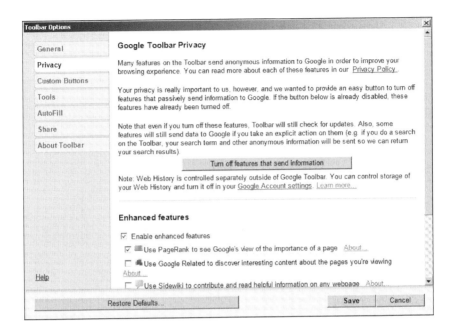

You need to select both Enable enhanced features and Use PageRank to see Google's view of the importance of a page. On some versions of the Google Toolbar it can be found under the General Tab as shown on the next screen shot.

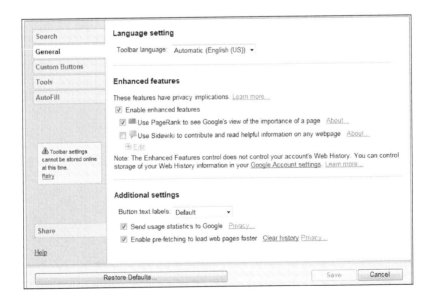

The Google PageRank is in essence the term *quality scoring*. Google's PageRank is a score of a website from zero to ten (0-10). Ten is the highest and zero is the lowest. Every website Google has visited has a score.

Google makes a ranking of a website based mainly on the factors such as how old a domain is, the amount of traffic over a length of time, and many other factors. The Google PageRank is one of the most secretive parts of how Google ranks a web page. It has virtually no factor in results anymore but it does seem to have a factor in how Google applies its different algorithms which I will discuss later in this book.

Features Available In The Google Toolbar's PageRank Tool

Now that we have installed the Google PageRank tool let's take a look at the tools features. The PageRank Tool has four main features. Let's take a look at each one. The first really cool feature is the rectangular box you can see right on the Toolbar itself in Internet Explorer. It turns the PageRank Tool icon in to a meter that fills with a green showing a graphical look at the PageRank of a website page every time you visit a new website or new website page. If you hover over the PageRank icon on the toolbar with your mouse, it shows you the site's Google PageRank as shown on the next figure.

You can that the website above has a page ranking of 9 out of 10 and the PageRank icon is almost completely shaded in with green. If you had a new website and a PageRank of 0 it would show barely a sliver of green on the left of the icon. Rarely do you see a PageRank of higher than 2 without great marketing or without professional SEO help.

The Cached Snapshot Of Page Feature In The PageRank Tool

The next feature of the PageRank Tool has two parts to it. This is where you can tell on any website when Google has come to visit the website page you are on. If you click the tiny little down arrow to the right of the PageRank Tool icon you will see the first of three additional options—"Cache Snapshot of The Page."

> NOTE: *In Internet Explorer there is also a fourth option called the "PIN BUTTON". If you do not see the PageRank Tool displayed on the Toolbar you can select this option to permanently keep the icon on the Google Toolbar.*

When you view the Cached Snapshot of Page option, you see a picture of the website when Google last came to visit. Along with a picture of the website, the time and date of the snapshot is also logged and is visible as you can see from the above screen capture. You also have one other important tool here. Notice to the right a little link that say "Text-only version." Click this and see what the spiders, crawlers, and bots really see

> TIP: *One of the good things about the Cached Snapshot of Page is that if you right click with your mouse and you choose View Source from the menu you will notice that the original HTML code from the website is there. Many times when a website has been hacked or a client was playing with his website and completely destroyed the page but saved over the original copy. I have actually used the original code from the Google Cached Snapshot of Page*

to recover the web page to its original coding. This only works if you do it before Googlebot comes to reindex the web page.

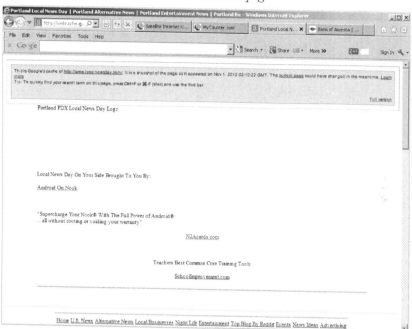

This is what Google sees and is actually the actual Text Only version of the first website you saw in the previous screen capture. It is incredible to see how little text relating to the website is found on this web page. All the text on the site is contained mainly in the pictures.

I have one customer who had the one of the best looking websites. It was all done in Flash. However, she had a page ranking of zero, even though she had the website up for 8 years. Her website was better-looking and more interactive than all of her competition.

Nonetheless, her competition was at the top of the organic searches and winning all the clicks, whereas she was not even found on Google because there was not a single word indexed by Google because the website was completely created in Flash. Google hates Flash.

Since the Panda also known as the Farmers update as it was called when Google's Algorithm, you need to have more content. The bare minimum is now 300 actual words in text on the page. The more words the better. The more recently updated and original the content, the better Google will index it and the better it will perform.

Once the company, that had their site done in Flash, became a customer, you can't even imagine how upset she was when I told her we would have to with JQuery and include text instead to get her rankings up.   It is hard for some people to understand why Flashy isn't always better.

Similar Pages Feature In The Google Toolbar PageRank Tool

The second option on the drop down menu of the Google Toolbar PageRank plug-in is the Similar Pages option as seen below.

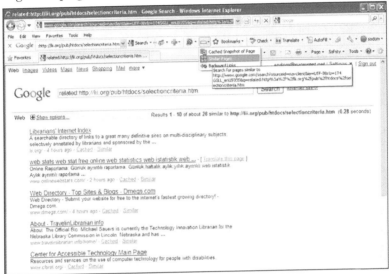

The Similar Pages option provides you with, not surprisingly, links to pages which Google deems similar to the products or services you offer your visitors on your website. These websites Google finds relevant because of the content you have on your website. Linking to these websites are prime candidates for link exchanges which we will talk about later in this book. Since Google already believes they are related to your industry. The more relevant the links to and from your website are, the higher Google will make your PageRank score.

> **WARNING:** If you see websites here that are not even close to the products and services your website offers, you need to either look at the wording on your pages or look at links coming from other websites to you. This is a good indication that Google thinks your website is in another industry and has misclassified your website.

Backward Links Feature In The Google Toolbar PageRank Tool

The Backwards Links option takes you to a list of links that the Googlebot has found that link directly to your website. These are very important to know because these are links that Google find absolutely relevant and indicate they are good links in Googles eyes.

The more of these from relevant sites that Google knows about, the higher your PageRank and positioning on Google's results can be. I am separating the two because PageRank and Google's results have very little in common anymore.

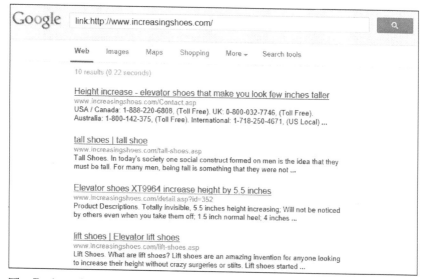

The Backwards Links option takes you to a list of links that the Googlebot has found that link directly to your website. These are very important to know. The more of these from relevant sites that Google knows about, the higher your PageRank will be.

Chapter 13– When You Need Professional SEO Services

After reading this book you may have come to the conclusion that you don't want to or have the time to invest on optimizing your website. Or maybe you have investigated the competition and found that the amount of competition is too much for you to handle on your own. Whatever the reason, you may come to a point where you feel that hiring a professional is what you need to do.

I could just stop the chapter right here and say hey, e-mail me at:

Sean@SEOForResults.com

We will take care of you. If that is not what you want to do, let me give you some pointers to help you out. There are a lot of scam artists, cons, and the like which want to separate you from the money in your bank account. In fact I think it is easier to find the scam artists peddling SEO than the real thing.

If I were to guess on a ratio. There is probably 100 scammers for every one SEO consultant that knows enough to get you listed at the top of the search engines. The information in this chapter is crucial to learn to keep you from falling victim to scams.

Hiring the Right Professionals

In this business cutting corners is not an option, because the wrong SEO practices can be far more detrimental to your website than doing nothing at all. Virtually everyone of my major clients was first scammed by an SEO scammer before coming to me. In fact, it is not at all unusual to hear about a company or website owner that's been scammed by a supposed SEO consultant who guaranteed them top placement in hundreds of search engines in just days and they actually sent the fraudulent company money.

One of the first clues is the absolute guarantee part. It's just not possible for anyone, even an SEO expert, to guarantee that your site will appear at number one of search engine rankings all the time. Nonetheless, many people claiming to be SEO experts will tell you they can do just that and in just days. Don't believe them. Good organic rankings for keywords worth using takes months to achieve.

In most cases, what happens is this: A website designer or owner who has had to create a website for SEO decides he or she can implement SEO for others to make a profit. However, just because these people have done SEO on their own sites doesn't mean they can plan SEO and implement optimization techniques on your website in the most effective manner possible. Every site, company and industry have different optimization needs.

In most cases, it takes a team of people to perform proper SEO techniques for a business website. That team might include someone to submit your website to different directories and search engines, someone to create and submit articles to online resources, someone to design and implement SEO elements, someone else to code the website to make it attractive to search engines, and a project manager to manage the whole SEO program from beginning to end.

Recognizing SEO Scammers

There are certain things you should check or look for when choosing an SEO company. These are the following:

- Get references from them. See where their customers rank. Go one step further, though. If at the bottom of the referral website's homepage it does not show that the SEO company you are checking out does their web design or SEO work, call or email the company and verify that their SEO work is handled by them.

  It is not uncommon for scammers to find a highly-ranked site and claim it is their work. In SEO For Results case, many of our customers allow us to keep a link at the bottom of their homepage that states, "SEO Services Provided By: SEO For Results" and a link to our page. It makes it easy for our customers to see we really do the work we say we do.

- Be wary if the prospective company says that they guarantee that your site will show up in the first page of results or even as the number one result every time! Time for a reality check: the algorithms that the search engines use are closely guarded trade secrets meaning that no one outside of a few people at the search engine companies knows exactly how it all works. Guaranteeing a certain page ranking is a sign of inexperience at best – and much more likely, indicates a scam.

- If you hear an obviously busy call center in the background, run. If their sales department is a room crowded with telemarketers trolling for business around the clock, it's a big red flag that you are being scammed.

- They promise to secure you top rankings for long-tail keywords which strikes you as unlikely to be used by anyone. For starters, they are trying to sell you a guaranteed page ranking (but we know better, don't we?). If the keyword they are offering you a top ranking for sounds a little fishy to you, look up its popularity with the free Google Keyword Tool we discussed in Chapter 1. See what its popularity is. Keywords that no one ever searches for are easy to main on page one of a Google search.

- If their services are offered at unrealistically low prices be weary. There are some SEO scammers who lure victims by offering to optimize your site and run promotional campaigns for prices that sound entirely too good to be true. Usually they want the amount upfront and from a checking account rather than a credit card.

- RED FLAG: "We can give your website and SEO tune up for $499.00."

- RED FLAG: "Results in 48 hours (or less). " If this could be done it would save everyone a lot of money and time. Everyone would be number one. Oh wait. They can't be.

Again, do your due diligence. Look at their credentials, find out who's used their services in the past and what they have to say about the company. You should expect regular weekly reports on how your keywords are performing and you should be able to easily get in touch by phone and speak to one of the SEO consultants to get their advice and input as needed. It needs to be an interactive process. If the reports are only monthly or quarterly that is not enough time to get notified when a keyword drops and take immediate action to correct the issue.

The best SEO companies have years of expertise in the field and know the most effective SEO methodologies inside and out. When algorithms change they also know how to determine the changes and react and have a process in place to notify their customers. Your placements on the major search engines may change from month to month but will return to normal as your professional SEO company does what is necessary to get you back to the top.

What to Expect From A Professional SEO Company

When you find an SEO firm that offers the services that you need, you can expect to receive certain specific services from them. The services vary from firm to firm, but here's a list that you can use as a good rule of thumb:

- You should be provided with an initial professional SEO audit. The audit should thoroughly examine your sites URL properties, current SEO elements, problems with the current design and structure of your existing website, provide keyword and competitor research, and look at the mechanics of a website as a whole and include recommendations.

- If you are trying to employ an SEO company that is a one man show who does the auditing, the optimization, the linking, the articles, the research, the social media, the web changes, monitors the analytics, does the billing, and everything else, you will soon learn that no one can be an expert at everything and you will soon be lost amongst his many clients.

  At SEOForResults.com everyone wears their own hat and focuses on just one part. That means there is a team assigned to every client.

- The company you hire should employ a project manager who tracks all the needs of your company's website(s) and follows the reports. This person needs to be able to bring in the experts needed at a given time they are needed and always be available by phone. If your SEO expert says he is only available by e-mail that is a red flag!

- You should be provided with recommendations for keywords and a plan to optimize your website. This report should indicate how each page of your web site is optimized including what on-page SEO elements such as HTML tags, keywords, and content needs to be changed on your website on an ongoing basis.

- You should be provided with information on how the SEO company plans to perform the optimization of the internal site navigation. Your internal navigation can have a serious effect on how your site performs in search results, so a good SEO will examine and optimize that navigation structure.

- Your SEO company should be able to scan the Internet weekly for mentions of your domain name in Blogs and other social media and provide this in a weekly report. This is now known as "Reputation Management" and is a critical piece of any online presence. And should be part of your weekly SEO Report.

- The SEO company should be able to scan your website weekly for design changes made that inadvertently broke links or strayed from the SEO goals set in place. These warnings should also be in your weekly SEO Report.

- A plan on how the SEO company intends to perform link building for your domain and verify they are only white hat techniques to sites relevant to your industry or follow guidelines set at http://angelasandpaulsbacklinks.com/.

- The company you choose should have procedures and the ability to test the different search engine algorithms to detect changes. They should be able to immediately make changes to your website to combat those changes.

- A plan on how the SEO company will show their progress and the monitoring of your SEO efforts and keyword statistics. They should also be able to give you statistics on your major competitors as well. If the SEO company cannot provide you this information on a weekly basis, especially in the beginning, find another company.

- SEO requires ongoing efforts. The SEO company must be able to train your staff with the most successful methods for maintaining optimization and providing news articles and suggestions.

Professional SEO firms can offer a lot of benefits to your website. After all, your core business is not likely SEO, but an SEO firm's is. The good ones can properly optimize your site, and your services, in less time than you can. For that reason alone, it should be enough to make you consider hiring an SEO firm, whether or not you end up doing so.

Chapter 15 - Educating Your IT Department or Website Developer

In most large companies I have come in to contact with over the years, the website is part of the Information Technology (IT) department and changes go through multiple layers of approvals for changes and the SEO company is usually hired by the Marketing Department.

Soon the Marketing Department is asking for coding changes and things that go completely against the nice esthetically pleasing website and friction starts to mount. One of the things must be done to create a good SEO campaign is changes to the on-page coding, keyword density, and many other aspects. It is impossible to do SEO without making at least some changes on-page, and that means eventually you'll need to enlist the services of the IT Department.

Even though we are working for the same, the SEO/IT relationship has historically been fraught with mistrust: you feel misunderstood, they worry you will break the website, and you're both operating with two very different ideas of what a "simple change" is.

Lend a Hand, Don't Reprimand.

Education is the best tool in an SEO's arsenal. Don't worry about guarding your preciously held secrets; we've come too far for that. most of the good stuff is stuff you won't need IT for anyway, am I right?.

It's easy for SEO projects to get stalled because not everyone involved understands what is going on or why it's important. Make sure IT gets an education in SEO basics (especially relating to site architecture/back end issues).

It accomplishes two things: it gives everyone a frame of reference for your future projects, and it gets a whole lot more eyeballs looking out for back-end changes that could have catastrophic SEO consequences.

Feel Their Pain.

You know how sometimes, someone wants results on an SEO project right away, and you are all like "You just don't understand how long that takes"? IT's life is like that, only times a million.

Be appropriate with your requests and reasonable with your expectations and you'll make everyone's life a lot easier.

If you get pushback on a project, work with the team to find a solution rather than going over their heads right off the bat. Same team, people. Same team.

Be Realistic.

Nobody expects you to be completely aware of all of IT's projects, but sometimes your changes just are not as important as other stuff they've got in the hopper – your title tag changes aren't going to get priority over a security flaw in your SaaS product.

Additionally, the benefit for some SEO tasks won't be worth the time and effort it will take to complete them, and you should try to learn and accept that when you have to.

That said, if there are things you feel are actively hurting the website, make sure everyone knows the ongoing costs of leaving them unfixed. If you can tie a dollar amount to it, you can bet it will get fixed eventually.

Be Available.

If you submit a list of changes and then wander off, don't be surprised if IT doesn't want to meet up at the flagpole after school anymore.

Part of being BFFs with IT is making yourself available for follow-up and clarification questions. Yes, as many as it takes.

Do NOT take the attitude that once you hand off the tasks to IT, they become IT's problem. If the site SEO fails because your project was implemented incorrectly, you will look bad, not IT. That means that your projects continue to be your projects and you're available to provide them with all the TLC they need until they're completed.

A Box Of Krispy Cremes Would Be A Good Gift Here

Make sure IT doesn't just see your face when you need something right away. Take some time to hang out with the team – bring cookies or doughnuts to their team meetings once in a while, get everyone out to happy hour, and then talk about the website.

This is a great time to revisit some of the SEO basics you have already taken time to teach them about. If anyone on the team expresses an interest in learning more about SEO, for God's sake make them your lunch buddy.

Sooner or later you're going to need a favor from these people. Wouldn't you rather be their pal who brings cookies than that needy annoying person from the Marketing department?

Give Them Tools To Help Them

This book is obviously a place to start but you can also send the I.T. Department articles educating them on why they need to make each change. Another item to consider is sending the person responsible to make the changes to a training class. I offer classes both one on one or in large groups. Visit **http://www.seoforresults.com/training** for more information.

Appendix A – SEO Checklist for New Non-Ranking Sites

If your new to SEO, I have created a quick little list to help you start ranking quickly. I have also included recommendations on how to make your website overcome each issue. Keep in mind that I am assuming you have already completed all the steps in Chapter 3.

Accessibility

Users and search engines both need to be able to reach all of the pages, you also need to make sure you don't have any dumb mistakes that can harm your SEO. These are things like 404s and 500 errors, and 302s instead of 301s, missing title tags, or thin content where there is not much material on the page for the search engines to grab on to and maybe for users as well. Get an AccuQuality.com or SEOAudits.com report done to help you eliminate these issues.

Keyword Targeting

Choosing the right keywords to target. You might not be able to target high value terms because you are also looking for low difficulty when you are first launching a site. You can look at search volume, the relevance to the website, and low difficulty.

Content Quality and Value

If you have users coming to this page and they are thinking this does not really answer my question or maybe only one part of my question, but I wish there was more detail. If you can change that to "I like this site, it makes me happy!" This kind of satisfaction from your users with the quality of the content that you produce, you are going to do much better in the search engines. Google has gotten so much better about noticing the true quality and value with results.

Design Quality, User Experience, and Usability

Unless you have a professional designer or you have a professional design background, you almost certainly need to hire someone or go with a very simple, basic design that is very user friendly. Then take a survey from friends and people in your company, see how they react to the site. Their reaction will tell you if the design works and if the usability is easy to understand. There is really no point in ranking unless you are nailing these two, because you are not going to get many more customers. People are just going to be frustrated by the website.

Social Account Setup

Because social and SEO are coming together like never before, Google is showing plus ones and things that people share by default in the search engine rankings. It really, really pays to be in social and social signals help search engines better rank things as well as having a nice second order effect on user and usage data, on branding, on the impact of people seeing those sites through social sharing and potentially linking to them.

For your social account set up you will want to have these four: Facebook, Twitter, LinkedIn and Google+. LinkedIn, Twitter, Facebook are all over 150 million users right now and growing every day. Twitter is at 200 million and Facebook is at 750 million, their numbers are growing quickly. While having your accounts spread throughout these social accounts you will want to keep them looking consistent so when people log on they know it is your site. Things like logos, colors, and photos help people to feel comfortable as they get to know you.

Once you have got these social accounts set up, you can feel good about sharing the content that you are producing through those social accounts, finding connections, building up in that world, and spending the appropriate amount of time there depending on the value you are feeling back from that.

Link Building

When you don't have any trustworthy quality links to boost you up, this is when low quality links can hurt your website the most. So, start with your business contacts and your customers to see if you can exchange links. If the contacts that you have in the business world are willing to say, "hey, my friend Steve just launched a new website, boom, that is a great way of getting a link". All your email contacts, your LinkedIn contacts, the people that you know personally and professionally, if you can ask them, hey, would you support me by throwing a link to me on your "About Page" or your Blog Roll or your list of customers or your list of vendors, whatever it is.

High quality resource lists are great too, this would be things like the Better Business Bureau. If you are a startup in the technology world, you definitely need to have a CrunchBase listing. You might want to be on some Wikipedia lists, it is a good place to start getting some visibility. Another great way is talking to the press, let them know when you are launching a new site or changing a branding, anything that could draw attention to the company and bring about publicity.

Social Media Link Acquisitions

This is where you spend time on Twitter, on Facebook, on LinkedIn, Google+ connecting with people and over time building those relationships that will get you the links possibly through one of these other forms or just through the friendliness of them noticing and liking, and enjoying your content. That is what content marketing is all about! All of this is very important and are really great ways to start, but they are not short-term wins. Most of these things require effort, investment of time, energy, creativity, good content, and some authenticity in your marketing versus a lot of the stuff that tempts people very early on. It is not like you will just go out there and instantly link up with 500 links and all of a sudden everyone is working together happily, there is much more work than that. Almost all low quality directories have spammy manipulative link profiles. Plus, they will not even show the brand names on the list.

Stay away from the low quality directories they will not help you with your business. You might want to also avoid article marketing or article spinning, unless you know how it really works it can hurt you way more than help you in the links world. One last thing to be cautious about are the forums, open forums, be careful of where you decide to leave a link. Google looks at sites that are grouping with a bunch of bad sites and will penalize them for their actions. A term for this is link farms, essentially this is when people are setting up all these different systems of links that point to each other across tons of domains that are completely artificial or link for no human reason, they are there merely to manipulate the engines, Google does not look onto these very nicely.

Appendix B – SEO Resources

There are many free resources for SEO on the Internet. Here is a few of them that I find most valuable, productive, or unique.

Best SEO Blogs

The world of SEO is constantly changing because search engines constantly change their algorithms. These blogs help you to keep up on the latest news, information, and tips about SEO.

1. Search Engine Land (SearchEngineLand.com) – One of the most well respected search engine and SEO news website.

2. Search Engine Guide (SearchEngineGuide.com) – A blog with a heavy focus on SEO for small businesses.

3. Search Engine Watch (SearchEngineWatch.com) – One of the oldest blogs out there.

4. Online Marketing Blog (TopRankBlog.com) – A great mix of SEO, PR, and social media articles.

5. Matt Cutts (MattCutts.com) – This is a blog by the head of Google's Web Engineering team. When he talks, you better listen.

6. Search Engine Journal (SearchEngineJournal.com) – This is one that I personally follow.

7. Google Blog (GoogleBlog.BlogSpot.com) - Google's official blog however they only discuss everything related to Google.

8. Traffick (Traffick.com) – A blog with a strong focus on PPC.

9. Google Blogoscoped\ (Blog.Outer-Court.com) – This blog is also all about Google. But the difference is, this one is written by a third party.

SEO Information Resources

Blogs can be your main source of information, however they don't cover everything. Usually the latest changes. If you are going to start from the beginning of SEO, here are some good resources as well as some unique resources.

1. Marketing Terms (MarketingTerms.com) – This site has a dictionary which will help you understand all of the marketing terms you run into.

2. Google's SEO Guidelines (google.com/webmasters/seo) – Google's take on SEO as well as their rules and a starter guide.

3. SEO Chat (SEOChat.com) – Here you can find a weekly SEO video and more information.

4. Search Engine Colossus (SearchEngineColossus.com) – Here you can learn that there is a lot more search engines than you may know of. This is a place where you can find them all.

5. Web Pro News (WebProNews.com) – Information and video interviews from SEO expert.

6. SEO FAQ (HighRankings.com) –This resource answers the majority of newbie questions.

SEO Tools

If you are not cheating and doing SEO right it is a very time consuming process. These tools will not only make your life easier, but they'll help you understand what you need to do and how to rank well on search engines.

1. SEOAudits (SEOAudits.com) – A tool to check your website for mechanics issues, browser compatibility, SEO issues and much more.

2. AccuQuality (AccuQuality.com) – Best website analysis tool I have ever used. They run 450 tests on every page which in include W3C compatibility, errors, code violations, browser compatibility, link problems, SEO, and they even spell check every page and provide a report.

3. Submission Complete (SubmissionComplete.com) – A very affordable tool to submit your website to all the major search engines and directories.

4. Website Submitter (WebsiteSubmitter.org) – Another affordable tool to submit your website to all the search engines and major directories.

5. SpyFu (SpyFu.com) – This site will help you understand what search terms your competition is using or is advertising with and how well they are doing.

6. Wordtracker (WordTracker.com) – You don't have to wonder how popular keywords and phrases are.

7. Google Toolbar (toolbar.google.com) – This toolbar will show you what your Google PageRank number is and much more. (See Chapter 1 for more information on to use this tool.)

8. Google Webmaster Tools (Google.com/webmasters/tools) – It seems this tool gets more and more important. You can now see the keywords people find your site with, errors on your website, submit an XML sitemap, and soon you will be able to see if your website has duplicate content somewhere on the Internet.

9. Digital Point SEO Tools (DigitalPoint/tools) – A collection of 17 different SEO tools.

10. AdWords Keyword Tool (adwords.google.com/select/KeywordToolExternal) – Although you might not be looking to pay for traffic, this tool will give you a good idea of how many clicks you can get from Google and help you with your keyword research.

11. DIYSEO (DIYSEO.com) – Tools to help you keep track of your SEO progress.

12. Backlink Checker (iwebtool.com) – See how many websites link to your website VS your competition.

SEO Forums

Sometimes you are going to be unsure of what to do. The best thing to do when this happens is to ask someone for advice. Through forums you can communicate with other SEOs or ask questions..

1. High Rankings Forum (HighRankings.com/forum) – A good community with a lot of friendly SEOs to help you.

2. Webmaster World (WebmasterWorld.com) – By far one of the oldest and well known SEO forums.

3. Digital Point Forum (forum.digitalpoint.com)– One of the larger forums in the SEO world.

4. Search Engine Watch (forums.SearchEngineWatch.com) – Almost 60,000 SEOs discuss search related stuff here. This is one that I use and highly recommend.

SEO Conferences

A good way to learn SEO is in person. Going to conferences won't just keep you up-to-date on the SEO world, but it will allow you to learn from some of the most successful SEOs.

1. Search Engine Strategies (SearchEngineStrategies.com)– Many conferences all over the world throughout the year.

2. PubCon (PubCon.com) – This conference started from the Webmaster World forum. Not only will you learn about SEO. It is held in Las Vegas and Austin Texas once per year. Usually November in Las Vegas and in Austin in March.

3. SMX – This is by far the largest of the conferences and are held all over the world.

Appendix C – IIS/.Net SEO Server Improvements

This part of my presentation deals with Microsoft's Internet Information Server (IIS) and how to improve technical SEO on the Microsoft server stack.

After completing technical SEO assessments on numerous sites running on IIS and .NET using both SEOAudits.com and AccuQulaity.com, I believe that it is a very scalable and production-worthy platform, but I have found that its default settings are far from optimal for SEO of any website that the server is hosting from a technical SEO point of view.

Oh, and here is a second caveat: Please be sure to test any changes on a staging server *before rolling them out* to production. I would hate for something to happen to your website because I made a typo, worded something unclearly, or these don't apply to your current configuration.

Default Pages (Default.aspx)

Directory pages are available at two different URLs, one with and one without the default page. For example, these two URLs would lead to the same page:

> http://www.seoforresults.com/home

> http://www.seoforresults.com/home/Default.aspx

In this example, the default page is Default.aspx, though it could be configured to be a different name.

To Google this is duplicate content. Google can get to the website on two different URL's. The same problem would be there without a proper 301 redirect if your domain came up by using www.seoforresults.com seoforresults.com. Inbound links to the page could point at either of these two URLs as well. You should focus all inbound links to a single URL.

No here is a .NET issue when redirecting one URL to the other. It sometimes leads to a redirect loop because both of these URLs look exactly the same to the .NET application. The default directory page is always automatically appended, so the application can't tell whether it should redirect the URL or not.

So how can I fix this problem? You should put a link **rel=canonical** tag on these pages and point to whichever URL you want to be the canonical.

It's not as good as a permanent redirect, but it will be one and in this case, you don't have to change your server configuration.

Creating Case Insensitive URLs

The issue with this, is the path portion of the URL which is served by IIS is case-insensitive. So any of these URLs will usually lead to the same page such as you see below.

http://www.seoforresults.com/home/default.aspx

http://www. seoforresults.com/home/Default.aspx

The fact that the case creates a different URL to Google, it creates a major crawler inefficiency. Google and Bing will crawl all of the different case variations that it sees in links and believe there is duplicate content on your website although all the links are going to a single web page.

So how do I fix this issue? Again, you can solve this issue by using canical tagging such as the rel=canonical tag that points to the URL with the correct capitalization or all lower case which I recommend.

I usually create a rule that rewrites the URL to all lower case that will work with a tool I use called URLRewrite:

```
<rule name="LowerCaseRule">

<match url="[A-Z]" ignoreCase="false" />

<action type="Redirect" url="{ToLower:{URL}}"
appendQueryString="true" />

</rule>
```

TIP: The Bing authorization file *BingSiteAuth.xml* is a case sensitive file name. You can add an exception for URLs which need to be case sensitive.

Error Page Responses in ASP.NET

The default configuration for ASP.NET handles errors such as if a page is not found by using only a 302 temporary redirect to an error page, which usually returns a 200 response.

A 302 redirect is only a temporary redirect notification to the search engines. This means they will continue to check that URL when they come to visit to see the new page when it finally appears. Some search engines still index the URL.

This issue also occurs if you have a server issue such as a database problem. In this instance many of your pages will default to the same 302 URL leading the search engines to believe you have a lot of doorway pages.

So how do I fix this issue? To fix this you need to modify **web.config** file. Here is code portion from the web.config file that prevents these redirects:

```
<customErrors mode="RemoteOnly"
defaultRedirect="GeneralErrorPage.aspx"
redirectMode="ResponseRewrite">

<error statusCode="404" redirect="404ErrorPage.aspx" />

</customErrors>
```

The attribute *redirectMode* needs to be changed to *ResponseRewrite* instead of its default value of *ResponseRedirect*.

NOTE: If the *redirectMode* option is not available, you will need to upgrade your version .NET.

Browser Dependent Code Issues

.NET has some features that makes it easy to rewrite the page code so that a page changes based on the user agent requesting it. From a technical SEO perspective this is a problem because it leads to unintentional cloaking of the content on the page. Google places penalties on any pages or sites that have any hidden content.

By default, there is nothing to fix. However, since this functionality is there, it is possible that browser-dependent code exists in your site right now.

How can I fix this? Well, tell your web developers not to use these code options on pages they create. But you should evaluate all the code for potential browser-dependent code issues.

Appendix D – Panda Vs. Penguin

Panda Vs. Penguin

The Titanic's Of Algorithm Updates For 2011 And 2012

During 2011 and through 2012 the biggest Google updates to their algorithm that decides organic placement of websites continue to change and scare website owners and SEO's alike. To some it seems hard to overcome the challenges these two algorithm changes create and some have found it stressful and hard to overcome. I speak all over the country at many industry shows and I open my forums up for questions. The number one questions from business owners and their marketing persons are what do I need to do to fix my website to get it back to where it used to be in the search engine indexes.

Google has made it no secret what you need to do to stay up at the top and if you follow Google's own Webmaster Guidelines you won't be hurt by any of these updates. If you are affected, understanding the reasons behind each update, helps to know how to fix your website if it is affected by Panda or Penguin or their updates.

The Panda Update

The Panda Algorithm and its many updates main goal is to get great content and get website owners to renew their content so it is fresh and rich. A second goal in the Panda update is to make sure that duplicate or similar content doesn't exist anywhere else on the Internet. Part of what

Google has had to deal with is people who visit their search engine not trusting the results they get.

Imagine you are driving in a car and you are going to a store to buy something. When you get there, you push on the door and notice the door is locked. You look through the window and you see nothing but trash on the ground because the company has gone out of business.

On the Internet, how do you know if a business has gone out of business? You may be buying something from a website that can still collect money but there is no one there to ship you what you ordered. It is a trust issue. Google wants to know you are still in business. It does this in a multitude of ways. First by knowing you recently refreshed or updated content on your website and an updated copyright tag with the year your company was established and the current year is just a start.

Copyright 2001-2013 (Make sure this is on your homepage.)

Next Google has proven it got smarter and wants to make sure your content is unique and not found somewhere else on the Internet. Google wants to make sure you know that you are not doing yourself any favors stealing someone else's content and putting it on your own website. Google will degrade the ranking or placement of both websites. A good way to check if you have copied or similar content from the Internet is o check your URL's at **www.copyscape.com.**

The Penguin Update

The Penguin update has a totally different focus. It targets those who try to pull the wool over on Google. If you have ever heard of "Black Hat" techniques for getting up on Google you know that those are techniques that violate Google's Webmaster Guidelines including those that try to SPAM Google. This can be many things including keyword stuffing, hidden text, cloaking, links SPAM, and much more.

Google has stopped checking for many items from their algorithms that Google virtually outlawed over the years. These items when they were checked for heavily were consider "Black Hat SEO tactics". Previously using those techniques could easily get you banned from Google and people stopped using them. Over time Google removed checking for some of those techniques in their algorithms most likely to concern processing power.

Overtime, some people realized by accident or by research that using these technique again actually helped their position on Google and there was virtually never a penalty. Word got around and people started using these techniques in huge number and probably praying this day would never come. The day when Google put the penalties back in their algorithm.

Keyword Stuffing

Keyword stuffing was one of the original optimization tactics and one of the first for Google to penalize. You want to put words on your websites pages that you want to be found for, however, when you put it 25 times in a row you get in trouble. In fact now when it is more than a few times in a row you can garner a penalty. As a rule you should never place the same text on a page more than once.

Hiding Text

There are several ways to hide text such as making hidden text by making it the same color as the background, making text to small, covering text with a picture using DIV tags, hiding text with Cascading Style Sheets (CSS), and many more. Those are just examples of the most common ways.

Google and other search engines don't like anything hidden on a webpage. Their crawlers want to see everything that a visitor sees. When a website owner places content just for the search engines, they're often going to extremes.

The general rule to avoid a penalty with the Penguin Update is to never hide text, whether by using styles, fonts, **display:none** tagging or any other means that means a typical user can't see it.

Cloaking

Cloaking is just sophisticated hiding. There are many ways to make the website How about rigging your site so that search engines are shown a completely different version than what the human visitors see?

That's called cloaking. Search engines really don't like it. It's one of the worst things you could do. While most people are unlikely to accidentally spam a search engine, the opposite is true when it comes to cloaking and Google gives a nice hefty penalty when you're caught doing it.

Unnatural Link Building

Tempted to run around and drop your links on forums and blogs all over the web, perhaps with the help of automated software? Don't do it and next, don't make your link building consistent. What do I mean by this? Say for example, you have a budget of $1,000 per month and you pay someone to build 50 articles with links per month creating a set amount of links each week or each month. When Google looks at your link growth, what they'll notice is that your link count is growing by the same number each month.

This type of is link growth is absolutely unnatural, particularly if you're buying all the links from the same source. It's easy for Google to notice this type of paid link building because Google is smart. Don't make it easy for Google to find a pattern in your link building.

Paid Links

These are links you pay for on a website or you pay someone to make for you. If you haven't heard the national news stories of JCPenney's or Overstock.com getting blacklisted for buying links you need to visit the NewYorkTimes.com and WallStreetJournal.com and read.

If you choose to ignore Google's Webmaster Policies and by links from overseas or pay to be on highly ranked sites which you are not contributing to or our in your own industry, be prepared for a quick death of your website in the search rankings. Buying these links will help you temporarily but when you are caught you will suffer. Don't believe these paid link websites when they say they're undetectable. They're not.

> **NOTE:** *Bing, officially doesn't ban for paid links, but it frowns upon such purchases.*

Exact Match Anchor Text On Links

Stop building exact match anchor links. It is now one of the biggest red flags to unprofessional SEO. If you are a plumber in Tampa and all your links say "Tampa Plumber" and link to your homepage, Google will eventually punish you. It's just not natural to have links that are an exact match anchor text to your website. You should be diversifying the anchor texts, focusing more on links that mention your brand name and less on links that mention have just your keywords in them.

Debunking The Panda And Penguin Update Myths

Since the Panda and Penguin updates came out I keep a log of virtually every persons opinion on what causes and effects these updates have had. In my own line of work as an SEO Expert I have to test and prove or disprove each of them. Let's take a look at each one of these and whether or not my research confirmed the title in bold or not.

Review Your Website Basics — Make sure robots.txt, XML sitemaps, search engine webmaster registrations with Google and Bing are up-to-date. *Research says..."Yes!"*

Duplicate Content — Get rid of duplicate content and check http://www.copyscape.com each URL you have on your website to make sure you no one has copied you. *Research says..."Yes!"*

Make sure your website is compatible with all browsers including IE, Firefox, Chrome, IPAD, IPOD, IPHONE and Android — If Google is going to rank your website highly it better be compatible with all the browsers out there. The only way I know of testing this is through either www.SEOAudits.com or www.AccuQuality.com. Not only do they show you if you are compatible or not, their reports also tells you how to fix each issue to be compatible with each browser. *Research says..."Yes!"*

Get Rid of Meta or other Redirects — You had Google fooled up until now but maybe Penguin is telling you that Google now knows about your hidden page redirects. *Research says..."Yes!"*

Stop Delivering Content Based on the Visitors IP Address, User-agent, etc. — Maybe your attempts to serve the best content to people by country are being misinterpreted by Google who thinks you are a spammer and trying to deceive people! Stop! *Research says..."Yes!" You will be penalized. If you want to serve other languages and countries get a domain form their country and host it properly.*

De-optimize the Website — If you have been "optimizing" your website with a high keyword density and over did it. Make sure your keyword density is around 6% and no higher. *Research says..."Yes!"*

Increase Good Links Pointing to Your Site — Make sure that they are from authority websites in your industry only. Don't use profile links or any link you have to pay for. *Research says..."Yes!"*

Add More Social Buttons — In normal times(The past two years) up until now a Facebook, Twitter, and blog link or widget would do just fine. This isn't the normal times I was talking about. Add GooglePlus, Google +1, and Pintrest. *Research says..."Yes!"*

Move Content to a New Domain — If you have been penalized by Google you can try and get Google to remove the penalties but research shows it is easier to start with a new domain and ignore the old domain. This time doing things right and in accordance with Google's Webmaster Policies. *Research says..."Yes!"*

Reduce Your Website Footprint — You think that by removing 800 of the 1,000 pages on your website will help you overcome the Penguin penalty....Myth. Add and keep adding good original content. *Research says..."No!"*

Write Better Content — Write human readable sentences that make sense. Start writing for humans and bots alike. Make the text make sense to both. *Research says..."Yes!"*

Stop Exchanging Links on Your Website — Absolutely not. Exchanging links is a great way to build rankings. But make sure each link has relevance. If you are in Chicago and you are a dentist, you can exchange links with other businesses in Chicago, other dentists, insurers, Chamber of Commerce, other medical doctors, etc. You are stretching it if you try and exchange a link with a car shipping company. *Research says..."No!"*

Do Not Use Low Quality Link Directories — If you have been easy-to-get-into directories, or making links using WP profiles you need to stop. *Research says..."Yes!"*

Remove Irrelevant Links to and from Your Website — If your site is about car shipping, you should not be linking out to Websites that are dealing with dental implants. *Research says..."Yes!"*

Decrease the Number of Ads On Each Page — If you have been placing a lot of advertising on each page and think this may be the cause of the Penguin update penalizing you, It's not. Don't remove the advertising. *Research says..."No!"*

Remove Your Sponsored Links — If you have been selling or trading a high volume of links to other websites and you were affected by Penguin update, get rid of your "non-contextual" links. *Research says..."Yes!"*

Get Rid of Spammy Backlinks — If you hired someone in India to give you 10,000 backlinks, Google wants to see them gone. Google will also call you out with messages in your Webmaster Tools account. Google is getting better and better at determining where links came from and the cheap links you can get from them have more negative value than positive in the long run. *Research says..."Yes!"*

Use Software Generated Content — Absolutely not! Google has figure out the article spinning software and will penalize you for using it. Get rid of it now! *Research says..."No!" Use real articles made by humans.*

Get Rid of Dead or Broken Links — Google is really looking at coding and broken links. More than a couple of broken links can be detrimental to good rankings on Google. You may want to get an SEOAudits.com or AccuQuality.com Report to find out how healthy your website really is. *Research says..."Yes!"*

Update Your Best Content Fequently — Refresh all your content pages at least every 90 to 180 days for best results on Google especially if it has not been done since last September when Google came out with a Panda update just to make sure content was refreshed. *Research says..."Yes!"*

Write Longer Blog Articles — Your articles are too short and have less than 300-500 words in them. Write longer blog articles! *Research says..."Yes!"*

Send A Reconsideration Request — A Reconsideration Request tells Google that you're really sorry you made or used bad links and that you will never do it again. It's a long shot but you have to do it or you'll remain in the penalty. *Research says..."Yes!"*

Appendix E - Click Fraud Click Fraud

Say you own a website that allows Google AdWords to appear on the site. Knowing you make a profit the ads are clicked on, you go to the site whenever possible and click on the ads. Cha-ching! Money in your pocket. This would be what is known as click fraud.

Sometimes click fraud happens when a person, group of people, or automated script clicks on PPC advertisements. Because the concept of PPC is that advertisers pay each time someone clicks on their ads, this drives the cost of ads higher and higher without resulting in any conversions.

Sometimes there is no immediate monetary benefit. For example, your competition might do it just to make your costs higher. Some advertisers also believe that PPC providers commit and even encourage click fraud to drive profits. This might not be so far from the truth. Several court cases have resulted in settlements when PPC providers such as Google and Yahoo! were sued for contributing to or allowing click fraud.

Unless all the clicks come from the same IP address, it's hard to prove that click fraud is actually happening. There are many software programs, called clickbots, that can create clicks from what appear to be spoofed or different IP addresses.

In many cases, there are indicators of click fraud such as an inflated number of clicks without conversions, clicks that all occur from the same IP, the same city, or if the time of clicks is unusual. These can all be signs of click fraud.

Another good indicator for me is when the level of clicks from Google partner websites are more than half the number of clicks on the actual Google search engine website. That is a big red flag for me and when that starts happening I know to turnoff the ads on affiliate websites.

If you suspect that you are being targeted by click fraud, immediately contact the fraud department of your PPC provider. If you don't receive satisfactory results from reporting the activity, then you should consider pursuing some type of legal action or discontinue the ads that are suspect.

Click fraud in the end can cost your company thousands, even tens of thousands, of dollars and ultimately destroy your PPC advertising campaign altogether. Only close monitoring of your stats for any signs of click fraud will help prevent it.

Look at this chart below. Because of constant monitoring we picked up on what appears to be an automated click fraud on day two of the fraud. Look at the figure. Can you tell the day?

We noticed the day this happened right away. We went to Google to see where they were all coming from and it was several affiliate websites. It was easy to see the huge increase in clicks. Halfway through the next day we eliminated the problem. It hurt initially but at least we didn't go bankrupt not knowing the problem was there.

Click Fraud Is a Crime

Click fraud is a crime, whether you are falsely inflating the number of click-throughs on PPC ads either for personal gain or simply as a way to harm the competition.

In an effort to insulate themselves from criminal charges and to create as many problems as possible, some advertisers will employ what are called "clickbots." These are software programs that search for and click on PPC links to drive up prices. These "clickbots" are usually automated and very often almost impossible to trace back to their owners.

Another form of click fraud are called "Paid-to-Read" searchers, also known as PTR's. Businesses actually hire readers to read and click through PPC ads online. It's much harder to track multiple individuals than to track a single individual at one location using repetitive activity or "clickbots" to commit click fraud.

Search engines are being made to answer for click fraud, and the associated costs that PPC users are having to pay because of it, causing search engines to crack down on the problem. If you get caught conducting a click-fraud scheme, you could face stout fines and possibly even a criminal prosecution that could result in jail time.

> **TIP:** I use a special tool called Click Report (www.clickreport.com) which report the IP information, where a click came from, and the keyword used to find it. It also lets me know when an IP has clicked on my ad more than once. I can then put that IP in to either AdWords or AdCenters IP Exclusion list to make sure that IP never sees my ad again

Index

29374697R00132

Made in the USA
Lexington, KY
24 January 2014